PROJECT SELECTION
AND
ECONOMIC APPRAISAL

PROJECT SELECTION AND ECONOMIC APPRAISAL

Wm. E. Souder, Ph.D.

Professor of Industrial Engineering and
Director of the Technology Management Studies Group
University of Pittsburgh, Pennsylvania

**Van Nostrand Reinhold/Continuous Learning Corporation
Series in
PRACTICAL MANAGEMENT FOR PRACTICING ENGINEERS**

VNR VAN NOSTRAND REINHOLD COMPANY
NEW YORK   CINCINNATI   TORONTO   LONDON   MELBOURNE

Library of Congress Catalog Card Number: 82-24859
ISBN: 0-442-21607-6

Manufactured in the United States of America

Published by Van Nostrand Reinhold Company Inc.
135 West 50th Street, New York, N.Y. 10020

in conjunction with
Continuous Learning Corporation
151 Erie Street, Cambridge, Ma. 02139

Van Nostrand Reinhold
480 Latrobe Street
Melbourne, Victoria 3000, Australia

Van Nostrand Reinhold Company Limited
Molly Millars Lane
Wokingham, Berkshire, England

15 14 13 12 11 10 9 8 7 6 5 4 3 2 1

Library of Congress Cataloging in Publication Data
Souder, William E.
    Project selection and economic appraisal.
    (Van Nostrand Reinhold/Continuous Learning Corporation
series in practical management for practicing engineers)
    Includes bibliographical references and index.
    1. Industrial project management. 2. Research,
Industrial—Management. I. Title. II. Series.
T56.8.S625 1983   658.4'04   82-24859
ISBN 0-442-21607-6

To Edie—she makes it all worthwhile

Series Introduction

Successful engineers are frequently asked to become managers. Although well-versed in engineering principles, many have had little opportunity to learn or apply management principles. For such professionals. Continuous Learning Corporation (CLC) has developed a series of educational manuals on engineering management in industry entitled *Practical Management for Practicing Engineers.*

The series is designed for the practicing engineer who has, or is in transition to, management responsibilities within an engineering function. Moreover, it provides the working engineer with the knowledge and practical techniques that are needed to solve engineering management problems in his or her organization.

The typical engineering manager has had three to seven years of engineering experience. His or her work may have been performed in a company's engineering or research and development department, or it may have supported the company's manufacturing, marketing, or field service activities. The engineering manager works at the intersection of engineering and other areas such as marketing, manufacturing, and finance. To work effectively in this capacity requires a thorough understanding of both the theoretical foundations and practical applications of managerial principles. Applying management principles demands skills in communication, leadership, maintaining creativity and motivation, quality assurance, and problem-solving.

Recognizing that engineering management demands a set of unique skills and attitudes not customarily acquired through traditional management training programs, the series is designed to cover the full range of subjects normally encountered by engineering managers. Included, for example, are treatments of these special subject areas: ideas, creativity, and innovation; project selection, appraisal, and management; technology of design and design practice; protection of ideas and knowledge; engineering organization, motivation, and career development; and quality engineering and management.

Practical Management for Practicing Engineers is designed for on-the-job use; the books in the series are also suitable for use as texts. Each book addresses a specific aspect of engineering management practice and is written by an expert in that field.

The focus of the series is on problem solving rather than theory. Case studies drawn from actual industrial situations demonstrate the application of management concepts and practices. Each book includes illustrations, examples, problems, charts and tables, and references to readily available supplementary materials. The objective of the series is to enable the engineer-in-transition to:

- Identify and analyze engineering management problems and the constraints within which they must be solved;
- Understand and apply effective engineering management principles and practices;
- Develop policies and strategies for long-term organizational performance.

Continuous Learning Corporation develops learning systems for post-secondary, professional, and industrial instruction. CLC's innovative courseware products utilize computer-based, computer-augmented, videotape, and print media for self-paced, individual, and classroom instruction. CLC performs needs assessments for prospective learning activities, conducts evaluations of educational programs, and provides a range of services related to professional and technical development.

Practical Management for Practicing Engineers was developed by Continuous Learning Corporation with the assistance of Robert T. Lund and Prof. Israel Katz, editors; and Alan Harger and Ann Davis, project coordinators.

KAREN C. COHEN, PhD
President
Continuous Learning Corporation

Preface

This book is of interest to all managers of engineering and research. It is very relevant for first and second line engineering and research supervisors: project managers, program managers, group leaders, section heads, department managers, and division heads. And it is especially relevant to the young engineer or scientist who is in transition to a position of managing an engineering or reseach function.

This book draws together the latest methods for selecting and evaluating engineering and research projects. Both qualitative and quantitative methods are included, covering the entire project life cycle from idea generation to project completion. This book can thus serve as both a reference guide and as a source of solutions to immediate management problems.

The author wishes to thank Mr. Robert T. Lund for his many valuable comments on an earlier draft of the material. Thanks also to Janine Valencik for typing the figures and tables.

Wm. E. Souder
Mt. Lebanon, PA

Contents

6. BASIC ECONOMIC APPRAISAL TECHNIQUES

7. ECONOMIC APPRAISAL AND SELECTION OF PROJECTS

8. PROJECT MONITORING, TERMINATION AND RESELECTION

1. Project Evaluation and Selection: The Problem

1.0. INTRODUCTION

A project is a system of jobs that must be completed within a given time frame and with a given set of resources [1]. A project often begins its life cycle as a nebulous idea for a new design, a new product, or a new process, and ends with the transfer of a developed technology to a customer or user [1, 2].

Engineering and research projects are "high leverage" types of projects, in the sense that their outputs or lack of outputs can have a dramatic impact on the organization's future. For instance, a successful project can lead to profits that are many times larger than its original development costs, while an unsuccessful project can mushroom into equally dramatic losses [2]. Thus, in the case of engineering and research projects, it is especially important to select only the very best projects, and to identify and screen out inferior candidates before committing significant resources to them.

1.1 THE NATURE OF PROJECT SELECTION DECISIONS

Project selection and evaluation involves the determination of the most appropriate or best ideas to start work on, and to continue working on as time passes. Project selection decisions are very closely interrelated with project funding and resource allocation decisions. For instance, the selection of a particular project usually implies some corresponding commitment of resources to it. Similarly, the selection of a portfolio of several projects implies something about the allocation of the available manpower and resources among these selected projects.

Project selection is also closely interrelated with project control: the assessment of the project's cost and achievement status as time passes. For example, any project that is not performing acceptably may be terminated and another candidate may be selected to replace it.

Project selection decisions are also closely interrelated with project completion and termination decisions. The completion or termination of an established project releases the manpower and resources that were previously committed to it. This may mean that another project can be selected, and work on it can be started with these newly available resources.

1.2 PROJECT SELECTION OBSTACLES

Project selection decision makers frequently have much less information to evaluate candiate projects than they would wish. Uncertainties often surround the success likelihood of a project, the ultimate market value of the project and its total cost to completion. This lack of an adequate information base often leads to another difficulty: the lack of a systematic approach to project selection and evaluation. Consensus criteria and methods for assessing each candidate project against these criteria are essential for rational decision making. Though most organizations have established organizational goals and objectives, these are usually not detailed enough to be used as criteria for project selection decision making. However, they are an essential starting point.

Project selection and evaluation decisions are often confounded by several behavioral and organizational factors. Departmental loyalties, conflicts in desires, differences in perspectives, and an unwillingness to openly share information can stymie the project selection and evaluation process. Much project evaluation data and information is necessarily subjective in nature. Thus, the willingness of the parties to openly share and put trust in each other's opinions becomes an important factor.

The risk taking climate or culture of an organization can also have a decisive bearing on the project selection process. If the climate is risk avoiding, then high risk projects may never surface. Attitudes within the organization toward ideas and the volume of ideas being generated will influence the quality of the projects selected. In general, the greater the number of creative ideas generated, the greater the chances of selecting high quality projects.

1.3 INFLUENCE OF THE TECHNICAL MANAGER

The technical manager—the group leader, the project manager, the department manager, or similar first line manager of engineering and research—necessarily plays a key role in project selection decision making. He is close enough to the technology to comprehend many salient technical details. But he also has a managerial perspective, as a result of his role as a member of the management team. The technical manager brings a uniquely integrated techno-business perspective to the project selection and evaluation process. (See Appendix A and Appendix B.)

1.4. NATURE OF THIS BOOK

This book presents the state of the art in project selection and evaluation methods. These methods are useful for reducing the obstacles to effective project selection, for increasing the organization's abilities to select only the best projects, and for eliminating inferior candidates. The principal audience for this book is the technical manager or the engineer in transition to the role of technical manager—the person who has major responsibility for creating, justifying, evaluating, and selecting ideas and candidate projects. (See Appendix B.)

Material in this book is presented in the order in which a total project selection and appraisal system should be designed, starting with the generation of ideas and ending with project termination. Chapters 2 and 3 present and discuss methods for stimulating and managing the flow of new project ideas. Chapter 4 presents methods for collecting and assembling project appraisal and evaluation data. Chapters 5, 6, and 7 discuss various systematic approaches and models for project selection decision making. Chapters 8 and 9 present some approaches for routinely applying project selection and evaluation methods on a continuing basis.

1.5. REFERENCES

1. Souder, W. E. "Project Selection, Planning and Control," in *Handbook of Operations Research: Models and Applications*, J. J. Moder and S. E. Elmaghraby (eds.). New York: Van Nostrand Reinhold, 1978, pp. 301–344.
2. Cooper, Robert G. *Project New Prod: What Makes a New Product a Winner?* Montreal, Quebec: Quebec Industrial Innovation Centre, 1980.
3. Souder, W. E. *Management Decision Methods for Managers of Engineering and Research*. New York: Van Nostrand Reinhold, 1981, pp. 1–11.

2. Identifying and Generating New Project Ideas

2.0. NEED FOR IDEAS

Few organizations have enough good ideas. There is always a need for creative solutions to existing problems, and innovative suggestions for new projects.

This chapter presents some methods for stimulating the generation and flow of ideas for new projects. Methods for finding new ideas, generating creative ideas, identifying opportunities, and managing idea generating groups are presented and discussed.

2.1. SOURCES OF NEW PROJECT IDEAS

2.1.1. Internal Sources

Most organizations have a variety of internal sources of new project ideas. The number and variety of ideas are limited only by the ingenuity of the personnel and the receptiveness of the organization to new ideas. Though the engineering, research and development functions are usually charged with the primary responsibility for suggesting new projects, good ideas should flow from all parts of the company. Ideation must not be viewed as the special province of one department. Marketing, commercial development, purchasing, production, and the other functions within the organization are also sources of new project ideas. These sources need to be carefully tapped and monitored, and provisions must be made for stimulating and collecting ideas from all sources within the organization. Subsequent portions of this chapter present some methods for stimulating and collecting internal ideas.

Table 2.1 Some External Sources of New Project Ideas.

Customers
Competitors
Suppliers
Purchase of technologies
Licensing of technologies
Unsolicited ideas from customers or others
Private inventors
Acquisitions
Trade fairs
Technology fairs
Private data banks
Technical journals
Trade journals
Government-funded research programs
Government innovation and technology transfer programs
Government agencies

2.1.2. External Sources

There are a large number of external sources of new project ideas. The traditional sources are the needs of the buyers, consumers, or users of the end product, and market research or customer contacts are the traditional methods for finding these needs. However, many other external sources also exist, as shown in Table 2.1.

One fertile source of new project ideas is competitors. Most organizations can produce similar products or variations of products which have been marketed by their competitors. Thus, a concentrated program that is aimed at watching competitors can often yield many new product ideas. For example, a well-known East Coast manufacturer of consumer goods conducted a study of patents filed by a competitor. The study showed that the competitor was building an expertise in several related technologies. Other studies confirmed that the competitor was planning to build facilities for a new product. Armed with this information, the East Coast manufacturer was able to plan and complete the timely introduction of a similar product, thus preserving their market share.

Table 2.2 lists five areas that may be routinely monitored for competitive intelligence gathering, as a basis for collecting ideas for new products and processes. A great deal of competitive information

Table 2.2. Some Areas to Monitor for Competitive Information on New Products.

Current Product Information	Production Information
• Product quality and performance	• Production capacity
• Breadth of line	• Facility location
• Product costs	• Capital investment
• New product developments	• Volume
Technological Information	*Market Information*
• R&D activities	• Pricing, discounts, volume
• Patent & licensing activities	• Market share
• Technical capabilities	• Distribution methods
Financial Information	• Advertising
• Sales	• Customer relations
• Profits and losses	• New market potentials and plans
• Operating expenditures	

is readily available from public sources in all five of these areas. These public sources include trade association publications, journals and newspapers, market research houses, patent statistics collection agencies, government analysts, business statistical and financial manuals, company annual reports and product specification releases, executive speeches, government publications, information vendors, and informal communication networks.

Suppliers are often a fertile source of new ideas. Suppliers can suggest many ideas for new products and processes based on their observations. They are in a position to see a variety of customer needs. For instance, a supplier of raw materials to a large Midwesttern chemicals producer remarked that one of their other customers was experiencing manufacturing difficulties. The chemicals producer investigated the situation, and determined that it was a common problem among many manufacturers. Based on their experience and technical expertise, the chemicals producer developed a new product that filled this need. Today, ten years later, that chemicals producer has over 95% of a large market which was unknown to them before a supplier suggested it.

Acquisitions and technology transfers are a frequent source of new products and new product ideas. Many companies often acquire other firms in order to gain new technologies and new products, and to enter new markets. Some organizations engage in the licensing or purchase of a variety of technologies and technological concepts as a source of new ideas. Many organizations find that private inventors and the citizenry often send them unsolicited ideas. It is not uncommon for some firms to search for inventors and small "garage-shop" companies that they can purchase, as a way of obtaining new technologies and the patent rights to new inventions.

Technical journals, trade journals, and manufacturers' advertising are traditional sources of new product and process ideas. Trade and technology fairs, where private inventors and small firms display their inventions, are a common source of new ideas. Recently, private technology and idea banks have become a prominent and fertile source of ideas. These idea banks are often computerized, and a wide diversity and number of types of ideas and technologies are available for purchase from these sources [1].

Government agencies, such as the U.S. Office of Technology Assessment, the National Science Foundation, National Aeronautic and Space Administration, and the U.S. Department of Commerce, are good sources of new product ideas. A number of government funded activities are also very good sources of new technologies and new product ideas. For example, Government funded research at universities, government research contracts, government innovation centers and government technology transfer centers are potential sources of many new ideas and technologies [1, 2].

2.2. IDENTIFYING PROBLEMS AND OPPORTUNITIES

A common approach to finding new ideas is to search first for problems, needs, gaps, and opportunities. Then, this information is used as the basis for generating new ideas, through the application of some of the techniques presented in subsequent sections of this book.

2.2.1. The Exception Approach

In the exception approach, a search is made for any deviation from the standard or the plan, or any deviation that may indicate the presence of a problem. The rationale behind the exception approach is that new ideas and new projects can be found by first identifying problems or gaps.

To illustrate, a manufacturer of heavy equipment makes a practice of assembling interdepartmental teams of personnel to investigate all major deviations from budgets and plans. These teams probe into the causes and influencing factors surrounding the deviations. A number of successful product improvement ideas have come from these activities.

2.2.2. The Deviation Check Approach

In the deviation check approach, a purposive inquiry is made into what is different, what is new, and what is changed from a prior period or a prior point in time. All deviations or changes are described in detail. Based on these descriptions, ideas for projects or programs may be suggested. Like the exception approach, the concept behind the deviation check is first to find the deviations, and then to use them as stimuli for generating ideas.

Table 2.3. Some Information Sources for Environmental Monitoring.

Thomas' Register of American Manufacturers. New York: Thomas Publishing Co.

Washington Information Workbook. Washington: Washington Researchers.

Business Trends and Forecasting Information Sources. Detroit: Gale Research Institute.

Directory of Directories. Detroit: Gale Research Institute

Statistical Abstract of the U.S.. Washington: U.S. Government Printing Office.

The Economic Almanac. New York: National Industrial Conference Board.

Survey of Current Business. Washington: U.S. Office of Business Economics.

Economic Indicators. Washington: U.S. Government Printing Office.

Predicasts. Cleveland: Predicast, Inc.

U.S. Industrial Outlook. Washington: U.S. Government Printing Office.

Census of Business. Washington: U.S. Bureau of Census.

Census of Manufacturers. Washington: U.S. Bureau of Census.

Quarterly Financial Report for Manufacturing Corporations. Washington: U.S. Federal Trade Commission.

Moody's Handbook. New York: Moodys Investor Service.

Wall Street Journal Index. New York: Dow-Jones.

Business Week Index. New York: McGraw-Hill.

Business Week. New York: McGraw-Hill.

The Wall Street Journal. New York: Dow-Jones.

Barrons. New York: Dow-Jones.

Forbes. New York: Forbes, Inc.

Fortune. New York: Time, Inc.

Dun's Review. New York: Dun and Bradstreet, Inc.

Harvard Business Review. Boston: Harvard Business School.

2.2.3. The Management Audit

A management audit is a deliberate search for opportunities. Unlike either the exception approach or the deviation check, emerging opportunities (as opposed to problems) are sought. A management audit consists of measuring, evaluating, and analyzing the performance of the organization vis-à-vis competition. Established performance standards must be set forth and used as a focal point for the audit. Interviewing methods, statistical techniques, financial audit methods and industrial engineering techniques are normally all used as part of the audit [3].

2.2.4. Environmental Monitoring

In this approach, various economic, social, political, and technological trends are constantly monitored and studied. Table 2.3 lists some common information sources that can be used in an environmental monitoring program. A comprehensive monitoring program would include information searching, data collecting, trend analysis, correlational analysis, and the application of a variety of methods for relating the observed variables and the factors found. Pattern recognition statistical programs would also normally be used. The objective of an environmental monitoring program is to search out and discover emerging needs, wants, and opportunities as a basis for suggesting new products [3].

2.2.5. Technology Forecasting and Assessment

In technology forecasting and technology assessment approaches, selected technologies are carefully watched for their growth or change over time. The objective is to forecast and assess those technologies which are the most likely to have the greatest impacts during the next few years. Based on these forecasts and assessments, new projects can be initiated to take advantage of emerging opportunities in a timely fashion.

A large number of technology forecasting and assessment techniques have been developed [3, 4]. Basically, two general kinds of approaches exist: modeling methods and expert judgment methods. Modeling includes the use of statistical trend analyses, and the fitting of various curves such as the linear, nonlinear, and Gompertz curves to base data for extrapolating purposes. Input-output methods, contextual chain techniques, cross-impacts analysis, and dynamic forecasting methods are also examples of typical modeling approaches.

The theory behind the expert judgment methods is that the collective wisdom of experts may be superior to individual viewpoints. This may be the case if a variety of perspectives can be collected and analyzed, thus bringing a total picture to bear on the issue. The opinions of several experts and knowledgeable persons can sometimes be "averaged" to cancel out the errors of individual predictions. Polls and panels of scientists are typically used in the expert judgment methods. In some approaches, the panel member's opinions are solicited in each other's presence. They are permitted to dialogue, debate, and exchange views as they please. Consensus is not necessary. Rather, what is sought is a diversity of viewpoints, perspectives, and predictions which can be further refined. In other approaches, the panel member's opinions are solicited under controlled conditions.

The Delphi method is one example of the controlled approach. The group is controlled in such a way that bandwagon effects, personality influences, and social group pressures are minimized. This is done by insulating the members from each other, so their opinions and identities remain anonymous. The forecast is arrived at through repeated rounds or solicitations, using a questionnaire. For example, in one Delphi, each panel member was asked to judge the date when a particular technology would be commerically available. In addition to supplying the date, each panel member was asked to write a short paragraph describing the basis or rationale for his or her predictions. The questionnaires were then collected and analyzed for statistical consensus. The mean and the standard deviation of the population of responses were computed. The short paragraphs were assembled into synopses. These statistics and synopses were then reported to the panel, and their predictions and opinions were again sought in a second round of questionnaires. These rounds were repeated five times, to achieve a consensus.

The keys to the effective use of all expert judgment methods are in the choice of the expert judges and in the choice of an appropriate problem [3, 4]. In general, where there is a great deal of uncertainty in the problem, where there are polarized opinions, or where much of the information is opinion-based, then the nominal-interacting (N-I) group process is likely to be a superior alternative method to the Delphi. The N-I process is described in detail elsewhere [3, 10] and also in Chapter 5 (Section 5.8).

2.3. IDEA GENERATION TECHNIQUES[1]

The latent creative potentials of many individuals are often blocked by various perceptual, cultural and emotional factors. One possible means for unlocking these latent potentials is to utilize some type of creativity or idea generation technique that aids in circumventing these blockages. A large number of creativity techniques have been developed [3, 5, 6]. Some of the most commonly used techniques are discussed below.

2.3.1. Brainstorming and Reverse Brainstorming

Brainstorming is one of the most widely used techniques for idea generation. The objective is to generate the greatest number of alternative ideas from uninhibited responses. Nothing is rejected or criticized. Any attempt to analyze, evaluate or reject ideas is prohibited during the brainstorming process. Instead, all ideas are written down for subsequent evaluation and development. The brainstorming session is usually carried out under a time constraint, e.g., develop as many ideas as possible in five minutes.

The group brainstorming setting is usually a lively session. Participants eagerly shout out and orally submit suggestions that are catalyzed and/or built on other ideas that are suggested. Thus, a chain of ideas can often cascade into unique items. Ingenious creations can be brought into existence as the direct result of the mutual encouragement of the group setting.

Reverse brainstorming (sometimes called the tear-down or purge method) may be useful prior to a brainstorming session, or in conjunction with other methods. It consists of being critical instead of suspending judgment. This initial attack effort is sometimes necessary to pave the way for serious efforts at innovative thinking.

---

[1] Portions of the material in this section are based on William E. Souder and R. W. Zeigler, "A Review of Creativity and Problem Solving Techniques," *Research Management*, Vol. 20, No. 4, July 1977, pp. 34–42, by permission.

Reverse brainstorming prepares one to deliberately go outside the situation to generate so called "idea hooks"—new viewpoints that are often quite remote from the actual situation. A typical approach would be first to list all the things wrong with the operation, process, system, or product. Then, systematically take each flaw uncovered and suggest ways of overcoming, improving, or correcting it. Care must be exercised to insure that the negative ambiance of a tear-down session does not completely overrule a group's optimism.

2.3.2. Synectics

Synectics operates like a mental pinball game. Creative solutions to a specific problem are sought through the two-stage process outlined in Figure 2.1. In the first stage, participants consciously reverse the order of things and "make the strange familiar," through personal analogy, symbolic analogy, and fantasy analogy [7, 8].

A synectics session is a lively and dynamic maneuver in which rational or obvious solutions are abandoned for what might seem irrelevant or bizarre approaches. Participants act like flints, igniting sparks in other members with their off-beat approaches. The intermittent involvement and detachment brought about by the analogies is subsequently culminated in a "force fit" to the original problem (Figure 2.1). Through the strain of this new fit, the problem is

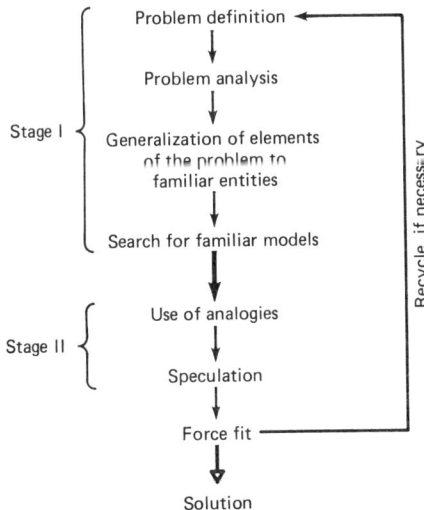

Problem definition

Problem analysis

Stage I — Generalization of elements
of the problem to
familiar entities

Search for familiar models

Recycle, if necessary

Use of analogies

Stage II — Speculation

Force fit

Solution

Figure 2.1. The synectics process.

stretched, pulled and refocused in order that it may be seen in a new way. A force-fit suggests new contexts and thus provides the raw material for new lines of speculation.

Prince gives an excellent example (see Reference 9, pp. 128–137) of the use of synectics to develop a bottle closure device. The problem was defined as follows: "to devise a thermos bottle with an integral closure." The generalization of elements of the problem to famililar entities (stage I, Figure 2.1) focused the group discussions around the concepts of "tightness' and "effectiveness of closure." The discussions generated several familiar examples of tight, effective closures, such as a clam's shell. The search for familiar models (stage I, Figure 2.1) swung the discussion to the concept of plastic closure, and the iris of the human eye as an example of a familiar model of "integral closure." The group then used elements of personal, symbolic and fantasy analogy (stage II, Figure 2.1) to speculate on the exact functioning of the iris and to apply this awareness to the thermos bottle problem. A force fit exercise was then undertaken, in which the group was directed to focus on the use of their awareness of the human iris to devise an integral plastic closure. From this exercise, the group suggested a thermos bottle with a rubber sleeve that would close as the top was twisted. One participant developed the key thought: "it's like twisting a long balloon at both ends; if you twist the ends in different directions, you close down the middle" (paraphrased from Reference 9).

2.3.3. Attribute Modification

In this approach the properties, basic qualities, or attributes of a product are listed. This list is then reviewed, one attribute at a time, with a view toward improving each attribute. For example, consider how the attributes of the common picture frame might be modified by applying this method. The attribute modifications are as follows. Rectangular shape: could be round, oval, trapezoidal, three-dimensional, continuous. Covered with glass: could be lucite, plastic film, nothing, a drawn shade. Wooden frame: could be extruded aluminum, plastic, no frame, built-in frame. Opens from back: could be a slot in top or side, hinge it to open from front, no opening at all, seal completely. Hangs by wire: could use suction cups, magnetic holder, hooks over a ledge [5].

Table 2.4. Illustration of the Forced Relationships Technique.

ELEMENTS: PAPER AND SOAP

FORMS	RELATIONSHIP/COMBINATION	IDEA/PATTERN
Adjective	Papery soap	Flakes
	Soapy paper	Wash and dry travel aid
Noun	Paper soaps	Tough paper impregnated with soap and usable for washing surfaces
Verb-correlates	Soaped papers	Booklets of soap leaves
	Soap "wets" paper	In coating and impregnation processes
	Soap "cleans" paper	Suggests wallpaper cleaner

2.3.4. Free Association and Forced Relationship Methods

Free association is a method of stimulating the imagination to some constructive purpose. The objective of this approach is to produce new combinations, intangible ideas, designs, names etc. The general approach is to first jot down a symbol—a word, sketch, number, picture—which is related to some important aspect of the problem or subject under consideration. Then, jot down another symbol suggested by the first one. Repeat and ad lib until ideas emerge. This technique can be used effectively by individuals or groups, with ideas "feeding" upon one another, often resulting in imaginative outputs [8].

The forced relationship method has the same basic purpose as free association. However, it attempts to force associations by the following five-step process: First, isolate the elements and possible forms of the problem at hand. Second, find the relationships between/among these elements and forms (e.g., similarities, differences, analogies, causes, and effects). Third, record the relationships in an organized fashion. Fourth, analyze the record of relationships to find ideas or patterns. Finally, develop new ideas from these patterns. As an example, Table 2.4 illustrates a forced-relationship analysis of the elements "paper" and "soap" [5].

2.3.5. Heuristics and Edisonian Methods

Heuristics are methods of demonstration and rules of thumb which tend to lead a person to investigate further. Some operational techniques based upon heuristics are: the techniques of close comparison of neighbors and similar cases; the examination of the simplest case; the examination of special cases; the search for a modified structure to which a rule applies. Heuristics are best suited to the detection of useful preparative material and problem elaboration.

The Edisonian method is an approach consisting principally of performing a virtually endless number of trial-and-error experiments. It is often considered to be a last-ditch approach, resorted to only when more systematic methods have failed to produce the desired results. But it is also useful when one is delving into unknowns, e.g., for exploratory work [5].

2.3.6. The Inspired (Big Dream) Approach

This technique is sometimes referred to as a breakthrough approach which can lead to spectacular advancements. It is predicated on the premise of "think-big." The procedure is: think the biggest dream possible. Then, read, study, and think about every subject connected with your big dream. Finally, drop down a dream or so. Then engineer your dream into reality. The objective is to make the greatest possible achievement [3, 5, 6].

2.3.7. The Gordon Method

The Gordon method is a technique for generating new viewpoints (idea hooks). It is used with a small group that is not initially made aware of the exact nature of the actual subject. The intent is to minimize preconceived ideas and habit patterns, so as to avoid a premature solution from being reached before there has been a thorough discussion of the general subject area. The Gordon method forces an unencumbered initial discussion that avoids the danger of a participant becoming so infatuated with his own solution that he ceases to be an effective contributing member. It also avoids inhibitions and/or prejudices that group members may bring to the problem that would adversely affect their performance.

The session leader, who is the only one knowing the actual subject, gets the group to think out loud about a related subject. For example, if the topic were to invent a new toy for a toy manufacturer, the leader might choose the topic "play" for discussion. He would first focus the discussion on aspects somewhat remote from the actual topic, then on aspects closer to it, and finally on aspects very close to the actual topic. At the end of the discussions, the topic is revealed to the group, who then analyze the tape recording of their discussions for possible idea hooks. Each idea hook is then brainstormed (or some other creativity method is used) to develop a final solution or idea [3, 5, 6].

2.3.8. The Sequence-Attribute Modifications Matrix (SAMM) Approach

The SAMM approach is most applicable to sequential situations where step-by-step activities can be listed and explored for possible creative modifications. An illustration of the SAMM technique is provided in Table 2.5, using an actual hot steel slab rolling operation [3]. The operating sequence of activities listed along the left-hand side of the matrix is examined for possible modifications. In the matrix in Table 2.5, the analyst has identified (with an "X") several priority areas to look into. For instance, the analyst has noted that the positioning and passing sequences (items 3 and 4) can possibly be combined and rearranged. The SAMM matrix does not describe how this is to be done; it simply identifies the areas. A number of

Table 2.5. An Illustration of the SAMM Approach.

Sequence/Attribute Description	Item No.	A (Eliminate)	B (Substitute)	C (Rearrange)	D (Combine)	E (Reverse)	F (Enlarge)	G (Reduce)	H (Modify)	I (Separate)
Heat steel slag to pliable state	1							X		
Transfer from heating furnace	2									
Position rolls to desired setting	3			X	X					
Pass slab through rolls (elongate)	4			X	X					
Check slag gauge	5					X				
Shear slab to desired length	6	X								
Transfer sheared product	7							X		

Key: X = possible priority items that can be modified, combined, etc.

other operational mechanisms, e.g., brainstorming, analogies, etc., can then be employed in the subsequent evaluations. This technique has proven more effective in group settings than in individual settings [3, 6].

2.3.9. Morphological Analysis

The morphological analysis method is a comprehensive way to list and examine all of the possible combinations that might be useful in solving a problem [3, 5]. These combinations may then be subsequently tested, verified, modified, evaluated, and developed. An example is presented in Table 2.6. The problem was to develop a low cost, fully portable, high validity color TV receiver. The four circuits (tuner, picture, sound, and color) could each be achieved in three ways: using all tubes, using all ICs, using all LSICs. However, at the time this problem arose, it was expected that the IC tuner and sound devices would not be perfected for another five years. As the analyses section of Table 2.6 shows, a compromise product had to be specified until the technology could be developed. The manufacturer entered the market with a less-than-ideal product, to be updated with a new model at a later time. It may be noted here that morphological analysis methods have also been used to identify emerging technologies and to forecast technical needs [3]. For example, the analyses in Table 2.6 point out the need for LSICs.

Table 2.6. Example of a Morphological Analysis.

| | | COULD BE PERFORMED USING EITHER: | | |
	TUBES	OR IC's OR		LSIC's
FUNCTION	TYPES:	TIME FRAME:		TIME FRAME:
Tuner	Pentodes	2 yrs.		5 yrs.
Picture	Pentodes	Now		5 yrs.
Sound	Pentodes	2 yrs.		Now
Color	Triodes	Now		2 yrs.

Analyses:
Lowest cost   = Pentode Tuner + IC Picture + Pentode Sound + Triode Color
Lowest weight = all LSIC's (5 years away)
Best validity = all LSIC's (5 years away)
Compromise = Pentode Tuner + IC Picture + LSIC Sound + IC Color

2.3.10. Means-Ends Methods

In means-ends methods, the repeated asking and answering of two questions provides a means-ends chain. To reveal each respective goal or end, the following question is repeatedly asked: "Why do I want this particular mean, action, program, or alternative?" To reveal each respective mean, the following question is repeatedly asked: "What stops me from achieving this end, goal, or objective"? Every end in the chain is a means to a higher end. And every mean in the chain is an end for a lower mean.

Means-ends methods reflect the dynamics of the iterative process of generating ideas. The decision maker often oscillates between problem statements and potential solutions before settling on a final solution. The means-ends process thus often results in some refinement of the original problem statement, along with many creative ideas [3].

2.4. MANAGING IDEA GENERATING GROUPS[2]

Successful scientists and engineers are often their own worst enemies in an idea generating session. Their training and prior successes may compel them to blot out things that seem silly, or that smack of irrational thinking and fanciful excursions. Yet these are the very practices that lead one down new alleys and passages that may culminate in creative new ideas. Participants in group ideation sessions are often surprised to listen to their own negativeness in tapes of their sessions. It seems a common trait to pay lip service to openness, and yet to rebuff new ideas. Thus, it is not unusual for participants to feel that group ideation sessions are boring and useless. The group often doesn't come to grips with the real problem, spends most of the time arguing about the problem definition, and generates criticisms of the ideas that arise. This effectively shuts off further ideation, and only bland ideas emerge. The individuals may go away feeling that they could have done better on their own. Yet, it has become clear that group settings can provide essential stimuli to creativity.

---

[2]Portions of the material in this section are based on William E. Souder and R. W. Zeigler, "A Review of Creativity and Problem Solving Techniques," *Research Management*, Vol. 20, No. 4, July 1977, pp. 34–42, by permission.

2.4.1. Structuring the Group

In order to achieve the best results, idea generating groups should be properly constituted, structured, and guided. Experiences indicate that the group should consist of at least one resident expert on the technology being discussed, one persuader, one confronter, one helper, and one dreamer. The resident expert supplies the depth of technological knowledge. The persuader has a friendly personality that persistently persuades the group to accept ideas and approaches on the basis of their inherent logicalness. The confronter has a bull-nosed personality that won't let anything remain hidden under the rug. The dreamer supplies the far-out, fanciful inputs. The helper maintains the group process, by periodically rephrasing and summarizing the work of the group and by occasionally smoothing ruffled feelings. The presence of each personality type in the group adds essential ingredients; each offsets and complements the other. The selection of these personality types can be an involved trial and error process, though there are several instruments that can assist in their selection [3, 10, 11, 14].

2.4.2. Providing Guidance and Framework

In addition to the members already mentioned, a process leader and a client should be present. These persons are not group members; they are outside helpers. The process leader is the expert on dealing with and guiding groups. He formulates the meeting plan and sets the framework for the operation of the group process. He gives the group corrective steering and feedback on whether or not they are being too confrontive, too passive, etc.

The client is the person who will use the group's outputs. He supplies factual knowledge to the participants, and provides the criteria for judging the "goodness" of the ideas which the group generates [3, 11, 12].

2.5. SUMMARY AND CONCLUSIONS

The generation of high quality ideas is a prerequisite to project selection decision making. This chapter has presented and discussed several approaches to the generation of ideas for new product and new process projects Methods for finding and bringing new ideas in from outside the organization, techniques for identifying existing new ideas within the organization, techniques for generating new ideas, and methods for managing idea generating groups were discussed.

The first level engineering or research supervisor, or the technical manager (see Chapter 1), can often have a significant influence on the generation and flow of ideas within an organization. In effect, the first line supervisor or technical manager is a "linking pin" between the creative engineer or scientist and upper management. He is the person most responsible for encouraging creativity and idea generation among his personnel, for properly communicating these ideas to upper management, and for transmitting top management's goals and guidelines into useful targets for the idea generators. Thus, the methods and techniques presented in this chapter may be especially relevant to the young engineering manager or the newly appointed first line supervisor. (See Appendexes A and B.)

2.6. REFERENCES

1. Ford, David and Chris Ryan. "Taking Technology to Market." *Harvard Business Review*, March-April, 1981, pp. 117–126.
2. Doctors, Samuel I. *The Role of Federal Agencies in Technology Transfer*. Cambridge: MIT Press, 1969.
3. Souder, W. E. *Management Decision Methods for Managers of Engineering and Research*. New York: Van Nostrand Reinhold, 1980, pp. 81–99, 137–162.
4. Martino, Joseph. *Technological Forecasting for Decision Making*. New York: American Elsevier, 1972.
5. Souder, W. E. and R. W. Zeigler, "A Review of Creativity and Problem Solving Techniques." *Research Management*, Vol. 20, No. 4, July 1977, pp. 34–42.
6. Van Gundy, A. B. *Techniques of Structured Problem Solving*. New York: Van Nostrand Reinhold, 1981.
7. Gordon, W. J., *Synectics*. New York: Harper & Brothers, 1961.
8. Osborn, A. F. *Applied Imagination*. New York: Charles Scribner's and Sons, 1963, pp. vii–viii (Preface).
9. Prince, G. M. *The Practice of Creativity*. New York: Harper & Row, 1970.
10. Souder, W. E. "Effectiveness of Nominal and Interacting Group Decision Processes for Integrating R&D and Marketing." *Management Science*, February 1977.
11. Souder, W. E., "Some Experiences with Idea Generation and Creativity Groups." Technology Management Studies Group study paper, University of Pittsburgh, Pittsburgh, PA 15261, June 15, 1975.
12. Souder, W. E., "Achieving Organizational Consensus with Respect to R&D Project

Selection Criteria." *Management Science*, Vol. 21, No. 6, February, 1975, pp. 669–681.
13. Souder, W. E. "Effects of Release-Time on R&D Outputs and Scientist Gratification." *IEEE Transactions on Engineering Management*, Vol. E-28, No. 1, February 1981, pp. 8–12.
14. Miller, D. C. *Handbook of Research Design and Social Measurement*. New York: McKay, 1970, pp. 200–212.

3. Managing Ideas and Developing Project Proposals

3.1. THE MANAGEMENT OF IDEAS

Chapter 2 presented a number of techniques for finding and generating new ideas. Though these techniques are quite useful, their greatest effectiveness is achieved when they are employed as part of a total system of idea management.

Idea generation is a complex, subtle, delicate human behavioral process. It can only thrive under an idea management system consisting of an effective organizational climate, an appropriate reward structure, and an efficient idea handling facility.

3.2. CLIMATES AND REWARDS

Organizations may use various reward structures and policies to promote the internal flow of ideas. Let us examine some of the most often used policies, as listed in Table 3.1.

3.2.1. Release Time and Sabbaticals

Many research laboratories and engineering departments have policies that enable individual scientists and engineers to be temporarily released from their assigned activites to work on their own ideas. In some companies, scientists and engineers are allowed to spend up to four hours per week (10% of time) working on their own ideas. In other companies, individuals with meritorious ideas are funded to work on them full-time, for as long as several months. At still other companies, individuals are granted various percentages of time to work on their ideas in parallel with their assigned projects [1].

Table 3.1. Some Policies and Reward Structures for Promoting Idea Generation.

Release time
Sabbaticals
Job rotation
Diversity of work assignments
Involvement of personnel in a variety of experiences
Providing guidance and guidelines
Idea award programs
Idea campaigns

In general, sabbaticals and release-time policies have been found to be highly effective. But they require care in implementation and administration [1]. The individual who takes release time for any extended period is necessarily drawn away from the mainstream of activities. The individual takes a risk that his or her idea will be a dismal failure, while the assigned work that he leaves behind will go on to be a major success during the sabbatical. Moreover, there is usually no way to assure that the organization will use the individual's idea, even if it is perfected during the release time effort. Thus, the individual who goes on release time may incur some career risks and "opportunity costs." Furthermore, in a manpower tight environment, a release time policy may become a frustratingly elusive target. Management may not feel they can afford the luxury of releasing anyone from the crush of current assignments [1]. On the whole, however, such policies convey a message that management is interested in fresh new ideas. This generally adds to a favorable climate for idea generation.

3.2.2. Job Rotation, Involvement, and Exposure Programs

Few firms have found the stereotypical approach of "letting the person run free" to be an effective stimulus to the generation of useful ideas. In those few companies where this laissez-faire approach has resulted in increased idea productivity, the ideas have not generally been found to be relevant, practical, or useful.

The most productive idea generators are often personnel who have experienced a diversity of work assignments and environments. Thus, moving personnel around the organization to develop their experience base and their total understanding of the company are important ingredients. Involvement in all phases of the work—the planning, the execution, the finalizing, and the transfer of the results to the user—also appears to be a key ingredient. When the individuals are exposed to all the aspects of the work, they are much more able to see the interconnections and interrelationships, and to find significant gaps and needs. Moreover, this total involvement is highly motivating. Most scientists and engineers want to generate useful ideas that will have a significant impact on the company. Involvement in all phases affords them the best opportunity for this [1, 2, 3].

3.2.3. Providing Guidance

Many organizations pay lip service to idea generation, but then fail to effectively communicate guidelines on the types of ideas wanted. Nothing is more disappointing and morale-sapping, to both the managers and the professionals, than to have a large number of irrelevant ideas being generated. Ideas that are generated in isolation from top management involvement or without a plan for their utilization are likely to lead to disappointment for all parties.

Thus, it is vital to the success of an idea generation program to have well-defined goals and guidelines. These should be equally well-understood by all levels of the organization. For example, there is no excuse for the professionals to be generating ideas for radical innovations that will take the company into new technologies, if top management and the long range plans are dedicated to incremental changes in the current product lines [1, 2].

3.2.4. Idea Rewards and Awards

Numerous kinds of tangible and intangible idea awards have been used. Awards for patentable ideas, for significant technical ideas, for cost-saving ideas and for product improvement ideas are common. The nature of these awards ranges from salary adjustments to certificates of appreciation. Some examples are listed in Table 3.2.

The merit of such programs is open to conjecture. Properly administered award programs have been found to enhance the production of useful ideas [8]. However, whether the award should be money or some intangible, the size or value of the award, who should confer

Table 3.2. Some Examples of Idea Awards.

Outstanding Innovation Award—up to $50,000 bonus awarded annually for ideas that significantly impact the company

Best Annual Patent Award—$500 plus certificate and/or plaque for significant patents

Most Creative Idea Award—up to $15,000 bonus and/or plaque awarded annually for creative ideas

Team Achievement Award—certificate and/or plaque or bonuses for most outstanding team efforts

Hall of Fame Room Award—recipients' pictures and list of achievements placed in a hall of fame room or corridor

the award, whether or not peers should vote on the candidates, how to decide when an idea merits an award and who shall get the award, what to do about co-inventors and other contributors, and how to distinguish major ideas from ideas of lesser potential—these are some of the difficulties in formulating and administering an idea awards program [8].

Some companies have found that the above issues are best decided by the engineers and scientists themselves. These companies have therefore formed rotating membership "awards committees" who formulate the policies and judge the ideas. This approach has a dual advantage. Through service on the committee, the professionals acquire an awareness of management's problems and perspectives in evaluating ideas. And, as committee members, they necessarily interact with other idea submitters and management. They thereby serve as two-way communicators and translators of needs, guidelines, objectives, and goals.

3.2.5. Idea Campaigns

Periodic contests or campaigns for new ideas may be staged. These can be directed at a particular need or a particular type of idea. An intangible or tangible reward may be offered as an incentive. If they are well-focused and well-planned, such campaigns can be highly successful. For example, a well-known consumer goods producer recently engaged in a campaign aimed at soliciting a name for a new household cleanser. Employees were given samples of the prototype product, told to try it out, and asked to submit their ideas. A panel of managers and employees was assembled to select the best ideas.

The winners were given their choice of a year's supply of one of the company's products. Nearly all the employees submitted suggestions for names, along with suggested new uses of the product. Numerous technical and nontechnical ideas were received for ways to improve the product, and many new technical ideas were received for related new products.

3.3. IDEA HANDLING AND PROCESSING

3.3.1. Human Sensitivities

Ideas are often very personal. Thus, it is a natural human trait to want to protect our ideas. It is equally natural to become emotionally charged when we feel that others, whom we may have entrusted with our ideas, are not properly handling them or caring for them. Most people feel that their ideas are fragile, undeveloped things that must be properly reared. Like the mother bear and her young cub, we often react when our ideas are threatened and endangered.

Thus, the "care and feeding of ideas" is a delicate and sensitive matter [1, 4]. It is every bit as important as stimulating the generation and production of ideas. Indeed, the two go hand in hand. For example, any idea campaign that initially results in many new ideas will quickly become extinct if these ideas are not expeditiously handled and processed [3]. What happens to an idea after it is submitted will have significant feedback impacts on the rate of generation of other new ideas. Idea generation and idea handling are two interrelated components of a total system. One is incomplete without the other.

3.3.2. Principles of Idea Handling

There are five principles that should be carefully adhered to in designing any idea handling system. Unless these principles are fulfilled, any idea generation system will suffer in its effectiveness. These five principles, listed in Table 3.3 are: confidence, credit, shelter, responsiveness, and fairness.

Confidence in the system is very important. If the idea submitters are not confident that their ideas will be properly handled and treated, then they are unlikely to submit their most delicate ideas. Yet these may be the most creative ideas. If there is a severe confidence crisis,

Table 3.3. Five Principles of Idea Handling.

Confidence of the idea submitter in the system
Credit for the idea goes to the idea originator
Shelter the idea from its natural enemies
Responsiveness of the system to the idea submitter
Fairness in judging the idea

no ideas will be submitted. Building confidence is often a matter of having an effective idea handling system that adheres to the other principles. However, there is much that a supervisor can do to assure the submitter that his ideas will be properly cared for and to inspire confidence in the idea handling system. If the supervisor maintains a positive, receptive posture toward new ideas, and makes a sincere effort to assist the submitter, this will significantly contribute to a sense of confidence in the system.

Every idea submitter needs assurance that he will be credited with the idea. There is an ever-present danger that the idea-inventor's name will become disassociated from the idea once it is communicated to others. Care must be taken that the inventor's name continues to be associated with the idea, and that he receives proper credit for originating the idea. In most cases the only credit the inventor requires is that others know the idea was his. Money and other tangible rewards may be of little real value to him. Peer recognition as a productive contributor may be the only key reward he seeks. If this is taken from him, he has nothing. Thus, the credit principle is a vital one. Credit may become a problem in an organizational setting, where the original idea may go through many evolutionary changes before it reaches its final form and embodiment [5].

All young ideas must be carefully sheltered from several natural enemies and forces that will destroy them. These natural forces include the human proclivity to reject the fanciful and irrational, and to engage in premature evaluations. Thus, an effective idea handling system makes provision for sheltering an idea. Sheltering can take many forms. For example, the idea handling system may have a pool of discretionary funds or seed money that the idea-inventor can use to support the further development, elaboration, and testing of his idea. Sheltering may take the form of coaching and counseling the idea-inventor on how to best get his idea accepted within the prevailing organizational culture. Or sheltering may take the form of a team of enthusiastic personnel, on whom the idea inventor can safely try out his ideas without the risk of prejudgement.

Responsiveness is an essential quality of any idea handling system. Nothing can be more discouraging to an idea submitter than to have no follow-up action at all taken on his idea. Every idea submitter deserves to have an acknowledgment that his idea has been received, and to receive periodic reports on its status. Nothing shuts off the flow of ideas faster than to have an idea simply vanish or become "lost in the system."

Fairness is also important. Every idea submitter must feel that his idea will receive a fair trial. What constitutes fairness may, of course, vary from one organization to another and from one person to another. Generally, a fair trial will not pit an idea against an unequal opponent, e.g., judge an embryonic idea for a radical new technology against an idea for improving the cost of an old product. A fair trial implies a complete, detailed evaluation of the idea, using criteria that are relevant for that idea [2, 7].

3.4. IDEA HANDLING TECHNIQUES

Table 3.4 lists several idea handling techniques. Let us look at each of these.

3.4.1. Idea Inventories

Many organizations maintain a running inventory of ideas, collected by periodically circulating various forms among the personnel or by staging idea campaigns. An idea inventory can have many uses. It can serve as a central file, to be retrieved and searched in response to specific idea needs. It may help to insure that all ideas are properly recorded and documented, so that they are less likely to become lost.

Table 3.4. Some Idea Handling Techniques.

Idea inventories
Idea clearing houses
Idea banks
Fitting teams
Screening teams
Review teams

And it provides the data base for monitoring and studying the idea generation productivity of the organization over time.

An idea inventory may make an important contribution to the development and embodiment of embryonic or unclear ideas. To enter an idea into most inventories, the nature of the idea must be fully spelled out and a short abstract must be written. This facilitates the retrieval and future use of the idea. The documentation process generally results in the idea being categorized by its salient attributes and characterized in a variety of ways. Thus, putting ideas into the inventory forces those managing the idea generation process to comprehend the ideas well enough to restate them for the data base, and to maintain more complete information systems.

3.4.2. Idea Clearing Houses and Idea Brokers

Many organizations have developed procedures for directing ideas from one department to various potential users and clients within other departments. These procedures need not be very elaborate. A comprehensive "want" list of the types of ideas and technologies of interest to each department may be kept. With this list, a central clearing-house staff can shuttle incoming ideas to potentially interested departments.

Clearing houses depend greatly on the abilities of the clearing house staff. The staff must frequently interact with the potential clients and stay up to date on their needs and wants, in order to be effective in interpreting the want lists. In effect, the clearing house staff serves as idea brokers. They attempt to match existing ideas with existing wants, and to encourage the generation of new solutions to emerging problems. Clearing houses and brokerage functions are most effective when used in conjunction with the idea inventories described above and/or idea fitting and screening teams (see below).

3.4.3. Idea Fitting Teams

Many firms often find themselves with ideas that are not relevant to the nature of their businesses, or that simply do not fit the company personality. For example, an employee conceived an idea for a novelty product while working in the development laboratory of a bulk steel manufacturer. The idea appeared to be technically sound, and an apparent market was at hand. But it clearly did not fit the company's current product line, distribution channels, or current marketing know-how.

One potential solution to such misfit problems is to set up in-house idea fitting teams. A fitting team operates somewhat like an idea generating group, and it must be similarly managed (see Chapter 2, Section 2.4). However, this is where the similarity ends. A fitting team's charter is to massage, bend, twist, and fit previously generated ideas to the company. The fitting team's role is to convert high quality but irrelevant ideas into high quality relevant ideas. Note that there is an idea generating aspect to this task, but the emphasis in operation is quite different from the brainstorming, free association, Edisonian, big dream, Gordon, and similar approaches used to mass-generate new ideas. Rather, reverse brainstorming, SAMM, synectics, means-ends, and attribute modifications approaches (see Chapter 2) are more commonly used by fitting teams. In fitting, the emphasis is on disassembling the idea into its components, then stretching or recombining these components into more relevant ideas.

Idea fitting is a complex psychological and group behavioral process that is not yet fully understood [2, 4, 6]. Fitting does not seem to be as natural a process as idea generation. Effective idea generators do not seem to be effective idea fitters, and vice versa. Fitting teams often oscillate between periods of high output and enthusiasm, and periods of protracted wandering and dejected introspection. Thus, fitting teams usually require constant positive reinforcement and encouragement. The group dynamics of a fitting team are often very subtle, and it is wise to have a group behavior expert present to help guide the team efforts [4, 6].

To date, the greatest success with fitting teams has been achieved when they have been composed of either five or seven members, meeting in a cycled nominal-interacting (NI) format (see Chapter 5, Section 5.8.1). In this format, one or more exercises like the SAMM, attribute modification, attribute listing, or reverse brainstorming methods are used during the nominal (N) period. The results are then discussed during the interacting (I) period. Like a generating group, the team membership should consist of one resident expert in the technology, one persuader, and one confronter personality type. Unlike the generating group, the fitting team should contain one person who is very strongly application oriented and pragmatic by nature. The team should also contain one person who reflects management's viewpoint and persective on the company's capabilities and future orientations. In some cases, where these guidelines were followed, dramatic results have been achieved by fitting teams [4, 6].

It is essential for the idea-inventor to be present when his idea is being fitted, because most new ideas are embryonic in nature, and often incompletely documented. They are likely to be incompletely revealed, and quite possibly misrepresented or misunderstood by the fitting team. In fact, this has happened repeatedly with fitting teams [4]. It is essential for the idea-inventor to be present to elaborate, explain, embellish and convey the full flavor of his idea to the members of the fitting team. Moreover, the experience of interacting and dialoguing with the fitting team is usually an enlightening and educational process for all parties. Insights into group dynamics, idea selling and evaluation processes, and project selection criteria are often gleaned by the participants. Furthermore, the idea handling principles of fairness, credit, confidence, and shelter require that the idea-inventor be present at the idea fitting session.

3.4.4. Idea Screening and Review Teams

It is important for new ideas to be screened for relevance very early during their life cycles. This is the fairest policy for the idea submitter. It quickly provides him with definitive feedback on whether or not the organization is interested, thus giving him a basis for deciding whether or not to proceed. This is a vastly superior alternative to permitting the idea submitter to invest further time in an idea that is highly likely to be rejected by the organization.

There are two keys to effective review teams: criteria and membership. The consensus list of criteria used to assess and screen the ideas should be simple but relevant (see Chapter 5, Section 5.8.2) and the system for rating the projects should be equally uncomplicated. Thus, any of the screening models and the QS/NI process discussed in Chapter 5 (Section 5.8) are suitable for use by screening and review teams. The team members who evaluate and assess the ideas should include representatives from the management, production, scientist, engineering, and marketing staffs of the company. This will insure that all the relevant perspectives are represented. It is important that the idea submitter be present at the screening session where his idea is being assessed. As in the case of fitting teams, the idea submitter must be present to interact with the group and convey the essence of his idea [2, 3, 4, 7].

3.5. FROM IDEA TO PROPOSAL

Ideas that pass the relevance screen or a review team should be formalized in a proposal. Formulating a technical idea in terms of a project proposal is a very important part of the whole idea generation process. The way in which an idea is packaged and sold is almost as important as the quality of the idea itself. Anyone who has a good idea must be careful to package and sell it, and effectively communicate it so its benefits are fully understood by top management.

3.5.1. Contents of the Proposal

The writing and preparation of an effective proposal is an inexact art. The way in which a proposal is written will, of course, depend upon the prevailing styles and culture of the particular organization. An example of one proposal format is given in Table 3.5.

Table 3.5. An Example of A Proposal Format.

Proposal for Funding for Idea A26

Statement of the nature of the idea
This is an idea for a prototype———, which will———.

Need statement
This idea will solve problems that have been experienced by———, fill the need for———, or satisfy the requirements for———, as defined by———or indicated by———.

Benefits
If successful, this effort will benefit———. The work may also have the following side-benefits:———. If this work is not undertaken, then———may occur, and opportunities to———may be missed.

Costs
The cost to complete———work will probably be no more than———. This involves the costs of———and related work. Subsequent work, such as———and——— should cost no more than———.

Resources
The following skill types will be needed:———.

Timetable and milestones
The work is expected to be completed according to the following timetable———.

As shown in Table 3.5, the nature of the idea, in its elaborated form, should be stated as the first item in the proposal. Then, the need for the idea should be carefully documented and prominently displayed. The need statement should *not* be written in technical terms. This means that the technical idea proposer, i.e., the scientist or engineer, is likely to need assistance from his colleagues in the marketing or commercial area. Successful proposals usually require the collective wisdom of several individuals. It is important to involve these other persons early in the proposal writing process. If the proposal is accepted by management, these other persons will play important roles in the subsequent project work. Involving them early in the proposal writing stage can be an important factor in obtaining their commitment to and their emotional involvement with the subsequent project.

The need statement should be followed by a related statement of the benefits that will occur if the project is selected and implemented. These benefits need not be stated in quantitative terms. In fact, quantification may be inappropriate if the idea is at a very early stage of its development. Rather, a statement should be made to show how the project fits the long range and short range organizational goals, and how it furthers the organizational missions. A statement about the potential regrets if the project is *not* undertaken is also important. In many cases, the benefits from doing a project may not be as great as the *regrets* from *not* doing it.

The need and benefits-regrets statements should be followed by estimates of the potential cost of the project. These estimates are likely to be very preliminary in nature. Dollar estimates may, in fact, not be feasible if the project is at an early life stage. However, attempts should be made to give some indication of the life cycle costs of the project. For example, if the project is undertaken, and if it succeeds, at what point will capital be required? Will a new plant have to be built? Will follow-on products and second generation products be required? What will it cost to service and maintain the product? These are important considerations for top management.

Some assessment should be made of the kinds of human resources that may be required throughout the life of the project. For example, it is important to estimate when a large manpower build-up will take place, and the skill types that will be required at various stages. For example, if the project is undertaken, and if work progresses on schedule, at what point should marketing personnel become involved? At what point should production personnel become involved? Will other personnel or supplies be required?

Finally, every proposal should have a time schedule. This schedule should detail the major milestones for each of the stages of the project. The timetable should include an assessment of the ways in which these milestones will be achieved, and the various hurdles that must be overcome.

Any idea that has survived to the formal proposal stage deserves care in presentation. The use of summary tables, checklists and graphs is helpful to the proper packaging and selling of an idea. Where possible, the idea should be compared to similar ideas that have been successful, and contrasted with other ideas that have been failures. This may be done in a summary checklist with tables and charts. The proposal writer should keep in mind the perspectives of his or her audience. Most readers will not share the proposer's specialized knowledge, nor will they be as emotionally involved. Their level of commitment, excitement and understanding will thus be on a lower plane than the proposer's. The proposer must attempt to generate enthusiasm, while being fair and accurate in presenting both the positive and negative aspects of the idea.

3.5.2. The Dynamics of the Proposal Process

The proposal writer should expect that the effective selling of his or her idea will be an iterative process. It has been said that the castle is taken only by repeated storming of the walls from various angles and with various means. This may not seem appropriate to the idea proposer, who naturally feels a keen sense of ownership of the idea. The proposer may feel that the idea is so good that everyone should fully understand it and quickly accept it.

The idea proposer must understand that those who must pass judgment will not be as familiar with the idea as he is, nor will they be as emotionally excited. Thus, his first effort is likely to be a preliminary proposal. Questions and challenges will be raised, and he will be expected to respond to them. Some of the questions may be viewed by the proposer as bureaucratic delays, and even unnecessary.

But the process of responding to these questions can add much to the proposer's understanding of his idea vis-à-vis the organization's needs and wants.

Thus, several rounds of proposing, re-proposing, adjusting, and readjusting the original idea are to be expected. The original idea may, in fact, go through a series of modifications that move the idea far afield from the original concepts. This movement may be vital, in terms of making the idea fit the organization, and in obtaining top management commitment to it.

3.6. ORGANIZATIONAL REQUIREMENTS

The techniques and approaches discussed above can enhance the idea outputs of any organization. However, they cannot compensate for ineffective organizational talents, communication patterns and objectives.

3.6.1. Mix of Human Talents

Having the proper mix of human talents and role persons is vital for idea generation and project selection. If the organization does not have enough creative scientists and idea generators, then there simply will not be enough ideas coming forth. If there are many new ideas being generated, but these ideas do not fit the organization, then there are not enough idea fitters or idea translators. If the organization has pools of unexplored ideas, then there are not enough coaches, or mentors, or "grand old men" in the organization.

Thus, a mix of human talents and role-players is needed to carry out the idea flow process. Personnel can be selected and trained to play these roles as part of their regular functions in the organization [9].

3.6.2. Open Communication

Since most projects will be interdisciplinary in nature, they will cut across many departments and many parts of the organization. The willingness of interdepartmental personnel to work together as a team, and to formulate projects based on embryonic ideas, is highly important. Unless the organization has this willingness among its departments, it is unlikely that it will be highly successful in project generation and project selection.

3.6.3. Criteria and Objectives

It is essential that the organization have a set of agreed-upon criteria for distinguishing candidate projects. Without criteria, the organization will have no proper means for distinguishing good ideas from bad ideas.

It is equally important that the list of criteria be closely related with company goals. Otherwise, personnel are likely to develop ideas that do not fit the organization. A consensus exercise, in which various persons throughout the organization are invited to participate in the listing, ranking, and rating of criteria can be used to establish a consensus set of criteria (see Chapter 5, Section 5.8.2).

Another effective approach is to involve personnel at the scientific level in a variety of standing task forces and committees for long range planning. The advantage of this approach is that the participants carry away a feeling that they have participated in the goal setting process for the whole organization.

3.7. SUMMARY AND CONCLUSIONS

Idea generation is influenced by many subtle behavioral processes and psychological variables. Encouraging personnel to generate ideas, to share and communicate these ideas, and to elaborate these ideas through the inputs of others are delicate behavioral tasks. This chapter has reviewed various organizational techniques, idea fitting techniques and proposal development methods that can help with these tasks. For maximum effectiveness, these techniques and methods should be used as part of a total idea flow and project selection system.

As noted in the Conclusions section of Chapter 2, the technical manager or first level supervisor's position places him in the idea flow mainstream. The ways in which the first level supervisor manages the ideas and suggestions of his subordinates can strongly influence the tenor of his department, and his personal future as an effective manager. Developing and maintaining effective idea management systems is a primary job responsibility of all first level supervisors, and all first-line engineering/science managers.

3.8. REFERENCES

1. Souder, W. E. "Effects of Release-Time on R&D Outputs and Scientist Gratification," *IEEE Transactions on Engineering Management*, Vol. E-28, No. 1, February 1981, pp. 8–12.
2. Souder, W. E. *Management Decision Methods for Managers of Engineering and Research.* New York: Van Nostrand Reinhold, 1980, pp. 81–99, 137–162.
3. Souder, W. E. "Effectiveness of Nominal and Interacting Group Decision Processes for Integrating R&D and Marketing," *Management Science*, February 1977.
4. Souder, W. E., "Some Experiences with Idea Generation and Creativity Groups," Technology Management Studies Group study paper, University of Pittsburgh, Pittsburgh, PA 15261, June 15, 1975.
5. Jauch, L. R. "Tailoring Incentives for Researchers," *Research Management*, Vol. XIX, No. 6, November 1976, pp. 23–27.
6. Souder, W. E. and R. W. Zeigler, "A Review of Creativity and Problem Solving Techniques," *Research Management*, Vol. 20, No. 4, July 1977, pp. 34–42.
7. Souder, W. E., "Achieving Organizational Consensus with Respect to R&D Project Selection Criteria," *Management Science*, Vol. 21, No. 6, February, 1975, pp. 669–681.
8. Turner, W. J. "How the IBM Awards Program Works," *Research Management*. Vol. XII, No. 4, July 1969, pp. 20–24.
9. Frohman, A. L. "Critical Functions for an Innovative R&D Organization," *The Business Quarterly*, Vol. 39, No. 4, Winter 1974, pp. 72–81.

4. Collecting and Assembling Appraisal Data

4.0. PREPARING FOR PROJECT SELECTION

Chapter 2 and Chapter 3 presented various approaches to the generation and development of ideas and proposals for new projects. Subsequent chapters present methods for appraising and distinguishing good ideas from bad ideas, and selecting the best ones. These methods depend on the availability of valid and reliable data, on the characteristics and potentials of the proposed ideas. These data include the likelihood of success of the idea, the cost and market potentials of the idea, and the capability of the organization to handle the idea [1, 2].

This chapter discusses the types of data and information that are needed to effectively appraise, evaluate, and select project ideas and proposals. Techniques are presented and discussed for collecting and assembling these data, in preparation for appraisal and selection decision making.

4.1. TYPES OF DATA NEEDED

In order to fully appraise and evaluate any new project idea or proposal, four basic types of data are needed on that idea. These four are: costs, benefits, risks, and suitability.

4.1.1. Cost

Several costs are relevant in appraising a new idea. The various costs to carry out the necessary research and development of the idea are key pieces of information. Some typical elements of the cost to research and develop a new product or process are listed in Table 4.1.

Table 4.1. Some Research and Development Cost Elements.

Research Cost Elements
Personnel—professional/technical
Personnel—technician
Laboratory equipment
Laboratory reagents and supplies
Outside consultants
Library materials and literature
Analytical tests and evaluations
Facilities and space
Computer time
Purchased reports and studies
Statistical services
Development Cost Elements
Personnel—professional/technical
Personnel—technician
Personnel—crafts/tradesmen
Materials
Fabrication
Equipment—one-time
Supplies
Facilities
Computer time
Design and drafting services

Research is that set of activities which identifies the new product or process and establishes its parameters and characteristics. Development is that set of activities which rounds out the new product or process and brings it to commercial readiness [2]. Thus, as shown in Table 4.1, though the cost elements within these two sets of activities are similar, there are several differences.

Though they are vitally important, research and development costs are often only a small percentage of the total cost to complete and market a new product or process. The cost to introduce and establish the new product or process in the market place may be many times greater than its research and development costs. These *marketing start-up costs* may include the cost of promotional outlays to establish the product and the cost of setting up the necessary means to distribute the product to the customer and service it.

The *capital and equipment costs* to produce the new product will also usually exceed the research and development costs. Millions of dollars of long term capital may be needed to finance the construction of a new plant or new facility for the new product. Thus, it is not unusual for a new project proposal to have many "hidden" costs within it. Often, a successful new product will create the need for late-life capital outlays and marketing expenditures that would not otherwise exist. These costs must be carefully anticipated and estimated, and explicitly taken into account as part of the appraisal process. In short, the *life cycle costs* of the idea should always be explicitly considered.

The cost to produce and market the new product should also be considered as part of the appraisal process. However, decisions may be needed on which costs to include and how to allocate them if there are *joint products*. This is the case where the new product will necessarily be produced along with one or more other products (by-products). This often happens in the chemical industry, for example. If these by-products have a market, then it may be reasonable to divide the total cost of production among all the products. But if the by-products are worthless, then their cost of disposal effectively increases the cost to produce the new product.

Cost allocations sometimes create confusion and difficulties in project appraisals. *Variable costs*—those costs that vary with the scale of work, the level of operation or the volume of output—are generally not difficult to work with. For example, hourly personnel are readily costed into project estimates, given the hourly wage factor and the number of hours needed. Problems most often arise in handling *fixed cost* allocations and "overhead" items like depreciation and salaries. A typical quandry involves the appropriate amount of the fixed cost or overhead to allocate to the new product, so that it bears its fair share of these costs. For instance, suppose the new product shares a facility with an old product. It then would seem appropriate to allocate a percentage of the facility's operating costs and depreciation to the new product. However, this could "rescue" an otherwise inefficient old product from appropriately being phased out, since its costs would decline by the amount of the allocation to the new product. Thus, considerable judgment must be exercised in allocating fixed costs.

In general, in making project appraisals, the relevant costs are *only* those costs which would be *new or different* if the proposed idea is accepted. Any current or existing costs that will not change should not be included in the analysis. Thus, data need not be collected on them. For example, in the above shared facility case, if the consideration is for the new product to be added to the old product line, the only relevant costs are those that are *new* and *attendant* to the new product. The way in which the operating costs and depreciation are allocated has nothing to do with the decision to accept or reject the new product. These allocated costs are irrelevant to this decision. The only relevant costs are the *attendant new costs*: those new costs or changed costs which the new product would create or bring into the picture. Much more is said about these aspects in Chapters 6 and 7.

4.1.2. Benefits

A new idea or proposal can have several different types of benefits. Some of these are listed in Table 4.2.

Market and financial benefits are often sought for most new ideas. However, the technical contributions can also be very important. Today's technical contributions may be tomorrow's financial benefits.

Some project ideas are primarily defensive in nature. They assist in the avoidance of *regrets*. As noted in Table 4.2, these types of

Table 4.2. Some Benefit Elements.

Market and Financial Returns
   Sales volume or dollars
   Market share
   Profits
   Return on investment
Market and Financial Contributions
   Cost reduction impacts
   Sales facilitation of other products
   Reduced raw material costs to other products
Technical Contributions
   Contribution to other products
   Contribution to science
   Contribution to know-how
Regret Avoidance Contributions
   Maintenance of current position
   Reduction of losses
   Avoidance of lost opportunity

projects may contribute to the maintenance of the firm's current technological or market positions. An example would be a product improvement project which is aimed at maintaining a firm's current market share.

Some projects contribute by reducing the firm's losses (Table 4.2). An example is a cost improvement project. Some projects are undertaken in the hope of avoiding an otherwise lost opportunity (Table 4.2). For example, a large industrial goods producer recently entered into a joint venture with a consumer goods producer to create a product for a rapidly changing consumer market. The industrial goods producer undertook the joint project solely to take advantage of the unique opportunity, which would otherwise have been lost [2].

4.1.3. Risks

Project risk is a complex topic [2, 3]. It is often confused with the concept of uncertainty. Uncertainty is a state of affairs in which neither the outcomes nor the likelihoods of these outcomes are known [2, 3]. By contrast, risk is a state of affairs in which the likelihoods of the known alternative outcomes can be specified.

Risk is usually taken to be synonymous with the probability of success of the project. Actually, it is more consistent if risk is defined as the probability of failure. Then, the more risky the project, the higher the probability of failure. We will use this latter definition of risk.

Table 4.3. Some Types of Project Risk.

Technical failure
Market failure
Failure to perform
Failure to finish on time
Research failure
Development failure
Engineering failure
Production failure
User acceptance failure
Unforeseen events
Insurmountable technical obstacles
Unexpected outcomes
Inadequate know-how
Legal/Regulatory uncertainties

Table 4.4. Some Suitability Criteria.

Similar in technology
Similar marketing methods are used
Similar distribution channels are used
Can be sold by current sales force
Will be purchased by same customers as current products
Fits the company philosophy or image
Uses existing know-how or expertise
Fits current production facilities
Research and marketing personnel are both enthusiastic about it
Fits the company long range plan
Fits current profit goals

Many different kinds of risk can occur in a project over its life cycle, as noted in Table 4.3. Thus, a major difficulty in collecting data on the risk of a project is deciding what risks are relevant.

4.1.4. Suitability

The suitability of the project idea concerns the extent to which the organization has the requisite skills, talents, and resident know-how to carry it to completion. Suitability also concerns the "fit" of the idea to the organizational culture and philosophy. For example, an idea for a new consumer novelty item that is made from steel might not be highly suitable for a firm that produces steel billets. The idea does not fit the firm's usual ways of doing business. Table 4.4 lists some suitability criteria for assessing new product ideas.

4.2. MEASURING AND ESTIMATING COSTS

Several techniques may be used to assist in cost estimation and data collection. These techniques include: learning curves, cost factors, cost estimating relationships (CERs), cost indexes, life cycle costing (LCC) and design to cost (DTC).

4.2.1. Cost Ratios, Factors, and Indexes [2]

One commonly used cost ratio is

$$C_B = C_A \left(\frac{S_B}{S_A} \right)^y \tag{4.1}$$

where C_A and S_A are the respective cost and size at one level of achievement, C_B and S_B are the respective cost and size at another level of achievement, and y is the cost-size factor. Values of y can be specified from a historical analysis of completed projects or by a rule-of-thumb. For example, take the rule of thumb that doubling the achievement increases costs by about $1/2$. Then substituting into equation (4.1) gives $1.5 = 1 \times (2/1)^y$, and $y = 0.585$. This value of y may now be used to estimate C_B for a new project of size S_B, given some typical data C_A and S_A for a completed project.

A cost index is a dimensionless number for a given time period. It shows the cost at that time, relative to a particular base year. In general,

$$C_P = C_r \left(\frac{I_P}{I_r} \right), \tag{4.2}$$

where C_P is the present cost, C_r is the original or reference cost, I_P is the value of the cost index at the present time and I_r is the index value at the time the reference cost was obtained. A cost index is usually a composite of n items, e.g.,

$$I_P = \frac{1}{n} \left(\frac{C_{11}}{C_{01}} + \frac{C_{12}}{C_{02}} + \cdots + \frac{C_{1n}}{C_{0n}} \right) \tag{4.3}$$

where C_{ij} is the cost of the jth item in the ith year, with $i = 0$ being the base year and $i = 1$ being the current year. Examples of some common cost indexes are the series of wholesale, retail, and consumer price indexes that are published monthly by the U.S. Bureau of Labor Statistics, the Chemical Engineering Index, and the Construction Engineering Index.

4.2.2. Cost Estimating Relationships (CERs) and Learning Curves

A simple CER can be developed by making scatter plots of historical costs and observing the relationships that are depicted. A more sophisticated approach is to apply multiple regression techniques to develop equations which accurately define the relationships [2].

In general, a CER follows the general form

$$C = a + bx_1 + cx_2^2 + \cdots + kx_n^n, \tag{4.4}$$

Table 4.5. Example of Results from Equation (4.5).

$k = \$1,000$

i	E_i
2	$800.00
3	702.20
4	639.80
5	595.60
6	561.15
7	534.50
8	512.00
9	492.85
10	476.41

where C is the project cost, a, b, c, ..., k are empirically determined regression coefficients, and $x_1, x_2, \ldots, x_n$ are selected factors that have been found to influence project costs. For example, the x_i may reflect the complexity of the design, the likelihood of failure, the amount of work to be completed, etc.

The amount of time or effort needed to complete a task will often decrease each time that task is repeated. This phenomenon was first noticed in aircraft manufacturing. In general, this phenomenon is called learning from doing, or simply the learning curve phenomenon [2]. A commonly found learning percentage (time or cost decrease with each repetition) is 20%. This establishes an 80% learning curve, which means that the second repetition will take only 0.80 of the time or cost of the first one, the fourth will require 0.80 times that required for the second, etc.

A negative exponential function adequately describes the learning curve phenomenon. The model is:

$$E_i = ki^f, \tag{4.5}$$

where E_i is the cost or time required to produce the ith unit, k is a constant, and f is the learning factor. The value of k is set to the time or cost required for the first unit, and the value of f is set to $f = (\log q/\log 2)$, where q is the learning curve slope parameter. When $q = 1.0$ there is no learning, and when $q = 0$ there is perfect learning. As an example, when $q = 0.80$, if the first unit required k man-hours, then the man-hours required for the fifth unit would be calculated from equation (4.5) as follows:

$$F_3 = k \, 5^{\log 0.8 / \log 2}$$

Table 4.5 presents the results of using equation (4.5) to compute the cost (E_i) of producing units two through ten ($i = 2$ to 10), when the cost of the first unit k is $1,000.

The total cost of an entire job consisting of repetitive operations to produce n units can be computed by simply aggregating the E_i values over all n units. If the learning rate increases or otherwise varies with different units, then the corresponding E_i values are computed with the appropriate varying values [2].

4.2.3. Life Cycle Costing (LCC) and Design to Cost (DTC)

In the life cycle cost (LCC) method, all present and future costs during the complete evolution of the project are estimated. For example, an LCC of the purchase of an automobile would include the original purchase price, the interest on the loan and all the operating costs during the life of the automobile. A comparison of two alternative automobiles on an LCC basis might result in a different preference ordering than a comparison based simply on their purchase prices [2].

In the design to cost (DTC) concept, the market price of a substitute or like item is the starting point for analysis. Working backward from this price by the use of cost ratios or industry mark-up ratios, the development and production costs of the item are deduced. This is taken as the base cost of designing for zero performance improvements. The cost of designing for a 10%, 20%, etc. improvement can then be estimated from this base cost number [2, 4].

4.3. MEASURING RISK

Risk is generally measured by probabilities. There are basically two ways of estimating probabilities: the objective way and the subjective way.

4.3.1. Objective Probabilities

An objective probability is the proportion of times an event has occurred out of the total number of times it could have occurred. Historical analyses may be used to establish frequency counts of past events, which may be converted to proportions or probabilities of occurrence. For instance, if 5 of every 10 projects have failed in the past, then it may be objectively claimed that the probability of project failures is $5/10 = 0.50$. In other cases the probability of occurrence of a particular event may be estimated by enumerating all the outcomes [2]. For instance, the probability of drawing an ace on a random draw from a normal deck of 52 playing cards is $4/52$ or 0.0769.

4.3.2. Subjective Probabilities

A subjective probability is an index of personal belief. For instance, a subjective probability number of 0.70 simply means that the individual feels the odds are 7 to 3 that this event will occur. A subjective probability need not relate to any objective probability whatsoever. In many cases where subjective probabilities are used, the particular event may be a unique event that has not yet occurred, i.e., the outcome of a new project. A subjective probability is an expressed judgment, based on personal experience and insights. The subjective probability number is an index, on a scale from 0.0 to 1.0, that reflects the individual's felt judgment that the event will occur.

Two different approaches have been devised for soliciting subjective probabilities: direct query and indirect solicitation. In the direct query, the subject is simply asked for a number. Indirect solicitation deduces probabilities on the basis of observations of a subject's decision behaviors. The choice of one approach over the other depends on whether or not the subject feels comfortable with it, the time and costs to train personnel in the use of the method, and the subject's depth of knowledge [2].

4.3.3. Probability Concepts

The probability that event e will occur is denoted by $p(e)$. The probability that independent events e_1 and e_2 will occur simultaneously is given by:

$$p(e_1) \times p(e_2). \tag{4.6}$$

The probability that e_1 will *not* occur is given by $1.0 - p(e_1)$. The probability that at least one of the events e_1 or e_2 will occur is given by:

$$1.0 - [1.0 - p(e_1)][1.0 - p(e_2)]. \tag{4.7}$$

To illustrate these concepts, let $p(e_1)$ and $p(e_2)$ be the respective success probabilities of two projects, project 1 and project 2. Then $1.0 - p(e_i)$ is the probability of failure of project i, equation (4.7) gives the probability of at least one of the projects being successful, and equation (4.6) gives the probability that both will succeed.

4.4. BENEFIT MEASUREMENT

4.4.1. Index Numbers

In one approach to benefit measurement, engineering value analysis and DTC (design to cost) techniques are used to calculate the value of some standard product, project, or model [4]. This value is then normalized to 100, and it becomes the index standard. The project whose benefit is being measured is then value analyzed relative to the standard project, item by item, and characteristic by characteristic. Its value is then assessed as some percentage of the index standard of 100. Index models, scoring scales, scoring models, and value contribution methods are often used in these comparisons (see Chapter 5). More sophisticated scaling methods may also be employed [2, 4].

In the subjective approach to benefit measurement, the value of the project is intuitively rated or ranked vis-à-vis some other project by a panel of judges. The Delphi technique may be used (see Chapter 2). Or various rating and ranking techniques, such as the pair-wise comparison or the successive ratings method, may be employed [2].

4.4.2. Objective Benefit Estimates

Sales, profits, return on investment and similar financial values are commonly used as anticipated project benefits. These values are objective, in the sense that they reflect real, monetized values. Their measurement, however, is often done subjectively, i.e., based on judgment and intuition.

4.4.3. Expected Values, Losses, and Regrets

The expected value of the ith project EV_i is given by

$$EV_i = p_i V_i, \tag{4.8}$$

where V_i is the value of the ith project, and p_i is its probability of success. The value V_i may be expressed in either subjective (index numbers, etc.) or objective (sales, profits, etc.) terms.

In general, if c_i is the cost of the ith project, then its net expected value, NEV_i, is given by

$$\text{NEV}_i = p_i V_i - c_i. \tag{4.9}$$

The NEV concept is often used in comparing projects that have different costs.

The expected opportunity loss is another concept that is often used in comparing projects. To illustrate, assume we have two investment alternatives, A_1 and A_2. Assume that if we invest in A_1, there is a 0.30 probability of a \$10,000 return. If we invest in A_2, there is a 0.70 probability of a \$5,000 return. Thus the expected return from $A_1 = $ \$3,000 and the expected return from $A_2 = $ \$3,500, so that A_2 is the better alternative. In fact, if A_1 is selected, we lose the opportunity to receive an additional expected reward of \$3,500 $-$ \$3,000 $=$ \$500. This is the expected opportunity loss of alternative A_1. In general, the expected opportunity loss of the ith project, EOL_i, is given by

$$\text{EOL}_i = p_k V_k - p_i V_i, \tag{4.10}$$

where $p_k V_k$ is the largest expected value for any alternative project. The expected opportunity loss concept is simply another way of looking at the comparative value of a project, relative to the others that are available.

The expected regret measures the expected total losses that could occur under an adverse outcome. For example, suppose it costs \$500 in fees to invest in A_2 and there is a 0.30 probability that the investment will yield \$0 return. Then the expected regret is 0.30 $\times$ \$500 $=$ \$150. In general, the expected regret of the ith project is given by

$$\text{ER}_i = q_i R_i, \tag{4.11}$$

where R_i is the regret amount under the worst outcome, and q_i is its probability of occurrence. Note that a regret is quite different from an opportunity loss. An opportunity loss results from an opportunity foregone. On the other hand, a regret is the total cost, the total amount lost, the total wasted, the total amount given up, etc., if the worst should happen [2].

4.5. INTEGRATING THE DATA AND ESTIMATES

Project appraisals will be much more effective if the appraisal data are integrated into a total picture. Let us now look at several ways in which appraisal data may be effectively integrated, in preparation for subsequent decision analysis.

4.5.1. Benefit/Cost Indexes

The benefit/cost index I_j is given by

$$I_j = B_j/C_j, \tag{4.12}$$

where B_j is the benefit and C_j is the cost of the jth project or proposal. When benefits and costs are measured in dollar amounts then

$$B_j = \sum_t B_{jt}/(1 + i)^t \tag{4.13}$$

and

$$C_j = \sum_s C_{js}/(1 + r)^s. \tag{4.14}$$

Here, B_{jt} and C_{js} are the dollar benefits and costs in some future time periods $t = 1, 2, \ldots, n$ and $s = 1, 2, \ldots, m$; i and r are the appropriate interest rates for discounting benefits and costs (see Chapter 6). In most cases, the benefits will occur later in time than the costs, i.e., the costs are incurred in order to obtain the benefits [2]. Hence an allowance is made in this model for the two different time horizons, t and s.

When benefits are measured in nonmonetary terms, e.g., index numbers (see Section 4.4.1 above), then B_j becomes an index number B_j^*. Combined monetary and nonmonetary benefit measures may be used, e.g.,

$$I_j = (W_1 B_j^* + W_2 B_j)/C_j, \tag{4.15}$$

where W_1 and W_2 are appropriately chosen weighting factors [2]. In general, any jth project that exhibits either

$$I_j = B_j/C_j < 1.0, \qquad (4.16)$$

or

$$I_j = B_j - C_j < 0, \qquad (4.17)$$

should *not* be selected [2, 5].

4.5.2. Decision Trees

A decision tree is a diagram that shows the decision points, the decision alternatives, the events, and the outcomes of a sequence of activities. An example is shown in Figure 4.1. Diamond shaped boxes represent decision points and circles represent points in time at which two or more events may occur. The decision alternatives and event outcomes are represented by branches in the tree.

In the decision tree depicted in Figure 4.1, either a low technology or a high technology product may be developed and marketed. The high technology product costs \$2M to develop (shown as $C_H = \$2M$ in Figure 4.1) while the low technology version costs only \$1M to develop ($C_L = \$1M$ in Figure 4.1). The cheaper low technology

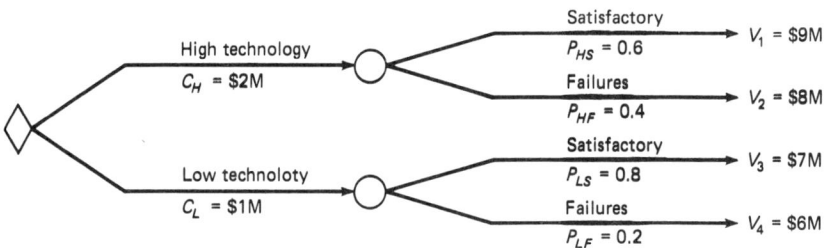

Key:

P_{HS} = probability that the high technology design will perform satisfactorily
P_{LS} = probability that the low technology design will perform satisfactorily
P_{HF} = probability that the high technology design will experience failures
P_{LF} = probability that the low technology design will experience failures
C_H = cost of the high technology design
C_L = cost of the low technology design
V_i = the market value (present worth of all future profits) of the ith outcome

Figure 4.1. Decision tree for the product design problem.

product has a probability of 0.20 of encountering field failures ($P_{LF} = 0.2$ in Figure 4.1), while the high technology product has a 0.40 probability ($P_{HF} = 0.4$). Because the high technology version has greater market appeal, its market value is estimated to be $V_1 = \$9M$ (see Figure 4.1). This may be compared with the $7M market value ($V_3 = \$7M$) for a satisfactory low technology product. Even if the high technology product encounters field failures, its market value ($V_2 = \$8M$) is expected to exceed the market value for a satisfactory low technology product.

Once the collected data are presented in this fashion, a very complete picture of the decision problem results, and several kinds of analyses are facilitated. For example, from equation (4.9), the respective net expected values of the high and low technology design alternatives are:

$$NEV_H = (0.6 \times \$9M + 0.4 \times \$8M) - \$2M = \$6.6M, \quad (4.18)$$

$$NEV_L = (0.8 \times \$7M + 0.2 \times \$6M) - \$1M = \$5.8M. \quad (4.19)$$

Thus, the high technology design is somewhat superior. However, based on equation (4.12), the low technology alternative is the superior design from a benefit/cost standpoint:

$$I_H = \$6.6/\$2M = 3.3,$$

$$I_L = \$5.8/\$1M = 5.8.$$

Based on equation (4.10), there is a relatively small margin of opportunity loss separating the high and low alternatives:

$$EOL = (0.6 \times \$9M + 0.4 \times \$8M) - (0.8 \times \$7M + 0.2 \times \$6M)$$

$$= \$8.6M - \$6.8M = \$1.8M.$$

However, it must be noted that this EOL is more than the incremental cost of the high technology design. The incremental cost of the high technology design is $2M - \$1M = \$1M$. Hence, it may be argued that the high technology design "pays its way." Thus, whether the high or low technology alternatives are chosen will depend on man-

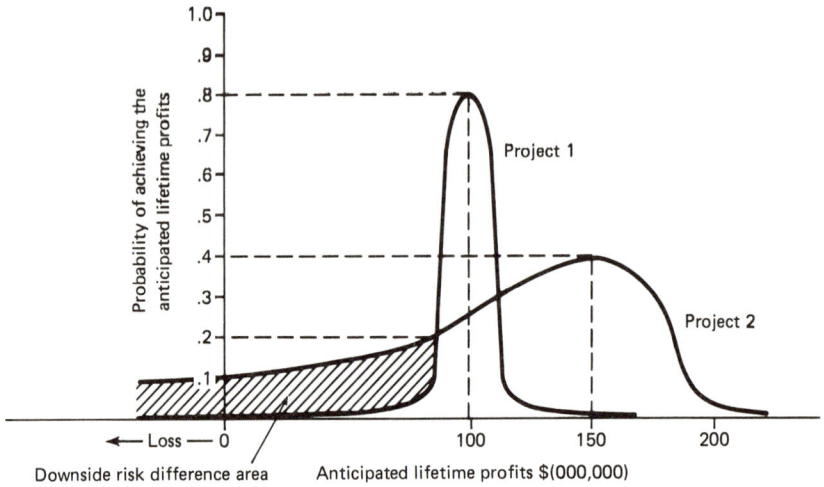

Figure 4.2. Illustration of a risk analysis profile.

agement's objectives and risk-taking propensities. The above types of analyses can help structure the data and make the decision alternatives more visible to management [2, 5].

4.5.3. Risk Profiles[1]

Figure 4.2 illustrates the perspective that a risk analysis profile can provide. Projects 1 and 2 exhibit most likely lifetime profits of $100,000,000 and $150,000,000, respectively. Thus project 2 might be considered superior.

It is not unusual for some analysts to terminate the appraisal at this superficial stage. But a much larger look should be taken at the whole picture. As Figure 4.2 shows, project 2 has a 0.10 probability of returning zero profits, and only a 0.40 probability of hitting its most likely $150,000,000 level. Or, as Figure 4.2 shows, there is a 0.20 probability that project 2 will yield lower expected profits than project 1. This is the relative downside risk if project 2 is chosen. Given these data, a risk averter would be inclined to select project 1. This project has a big chance of achieving a moderate profit, with very little chance of

---

[1] Portions of the material in this section are taken from William E. Souder, "A System for Using R&D Project Evaluation Methods," *Research Management*, Vol. 21, No. 5, September 1978, pp. 29–37, by permission.

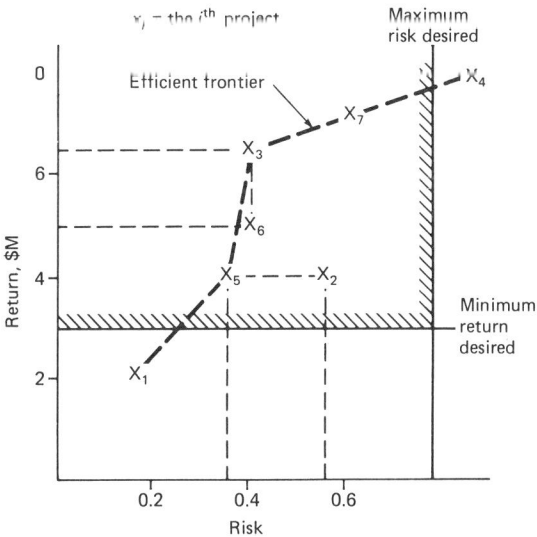

Figure 4.3. Illustration of a frontier model.

anything less or greater. A gambler would be inclined to opt for project 2, which has a small chance at a large profit.

Thus, risk analysis profiles make the risk-averter and gambler strategies more visible, thereby permitting a decision maker to consciously select decisions consistent with one of these chosen strategies. Generally, the amount of data needed to develop a picture like Figure 4.2 is not overly difficult to obtain. The data can be collected by direct solicitation from marketing and engineering personnel who are familiar with the projects [2, 5].

4.5.4. Risk-Return Tradeoffs[2]

Figure 4.3 illustrates a typical frontier model plot for six proposed projects. Though the definitions can vary with the particular model, *risk* usually expresses the project's chances of failure and *return* expresses its expected profitability. In Figure 4.3 the "efficient frontier" traces the path of the dominant projects. For instance, project

[2] Portions of the material in this section are taken from William E. Souder, "A System for Using R&D Project Evaluation Methods," *Research Management*, Vol. 21, No. 5, September 1978, pp. 29–37, by permission.

3 (denoted as X_3 in Figure 4.3) is dominant over project 6 (denoted as X_6). Project 3 has the same risk level as project 6, but it has a higher return. Similarly, project 5 is dominant over project 2. The maximum desired risk and the minimum desired return levels established by the organization are also depicted in Figure 4.3. Acceptable projects must fall in the region formed by these boundaries. Thus, Figure 4.3 shows that a decision maker would accept only projects 2, 3, 5, 6, and 7.

Frontier models are often very useful for examining return-risk trade-offs within the organizational objectives. For instance, Figure 4.3 shows that the high risk and high return project 4 is ruled out by its high risk level. Yet its incremental return/risk ratio is the same as the acceptable projects 3 and 7. All three projects lie on the same line. Thus, the decision maker may want to make an exception and retain project 4 for further study and analyses. Frontier models may also be used to indicate the need for greater diversification in idea generation and project proposals. For example, Figure 4.3 shows that the acceptable projects are primarily of the medium to high-risk variety. Whether or not the portfolio ought to be more diversified must be resolved by management on the basis of the organization's goals and objectives. The frontier model can only point out trends and situations for further analysis [1, 2, 3, 5].

4.6. SENSITIVITY AND INDIFFERENCE ANALYSES

The sensitivity of all appraisal data and changes in the premises and underlying assumptions should always be carefully checked in "what if?" exercises. To illustrate, let us check the sensitivity of the superiority of the high technology alternative in the decision tree example of Section 4.5.2, using the NEV criterion.

Recall that the NEV of the high technology alternative was $\text{NEV}_H = \$6.6\text{M}$, as opposed to $\text{NEV}_L = \$5.8\text{M}$ for the low technology alternative, as seen from equations (4.18) and (4.19). Will the high technology alternative always be superior, or *globally dominant*, to the low technology alternative on the NEV criterion, no matter what the values of $P_{HS}, P_{HF}, P_{LS}, P_{LF}$? If the high technology alternative is not globally dominant, then there will be one or more values of $P_{HS}, P_{HF}, P_{LS},$ and P_{LF} such that

$$\text{NEV}_H = \text{NEV}_L \qquad (4.20)$$

or such that

$$\$9MP_{HS} + \$8MP_{HF} - \$2M = \$7MP_{LS} + \$6MP_{LF} - \$1M. \quad (4.21)$$

Substituting the following identities

$$P_{HS} = 1 - P_{HF} \quad (4.22)$$

$$P_{LS} = 1 - P_{LF} \quad (4.23)$$

into equation (4.21) and solving we find the solution

$$P_{HF} = P_{LF} - 1,$$

which cannot exist. Hence, there are no values of P_{HS}, P_{HF}, P_{LS}, and P_{LF} that satisfy equation (4.21), i.e., that make NEV_H and NEV_L equal.

Thus, the high technology alternative is indeed globally dominant on the NEV criterion. This can also be readily seen by graphing the NEV_H and NEV_L equations (4.18) and (4.19), as illustrated in Figure 4.4. This type of analysis is also called an *indifference analysis*, since it seeks to find that point (if it exists) where the decision maker becomes indifferent about the choice of one alternative over another.

To illustrate the indifference point, let us test the sensitivity of the

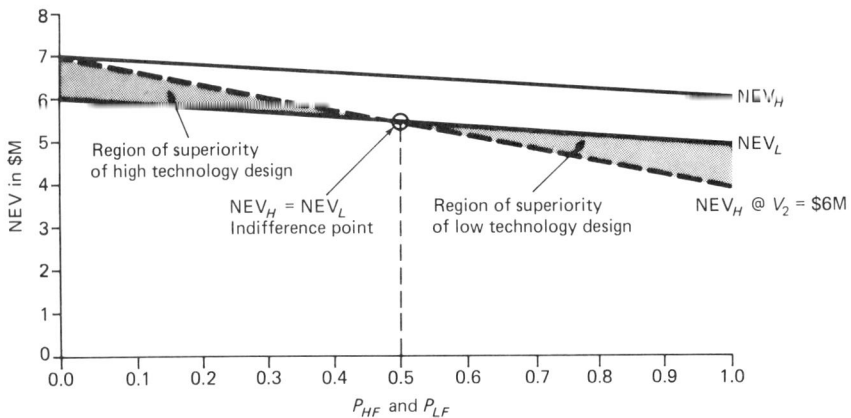

Figure 4.4. Dominance check.

above NEV results to changes in the magnitude of V_2 by letting $V_2 =$ $6M. Then equation (4.21) becomes

$$\$9M P_{HS} + \$6M P_{HF} - \$2M = \$7M P_{LS} + \$6M P_{LF} - \$1M,$$

and solving yields

$$P_{HF} = P_{LF} = 0.50.$$

Thus, an indifference point occurs when the probability of success of the high technology is 0.50 and the probability of success of the low technology is also 0.50. When the probabilities are 0.50, $NEV_H = NEV_L$, and there is no basis for preferring one alternative design over the other. This result is shown in Figure 4.4 by the intersection of the lines labeled NEV_L and NEV_H at $V_2 = \$6M$.

Figure 4.4 also shows that if P_{HF} and P_{LF} are less than 0.50, then the high technology is superior on NEV. But if P_{HF} and P_{LF} are greater than 0.50, the low technology gives the superior NEV. Hence, it may be said that the high technology is the best choice when mother nature is benign, while the low technology is the best choice when mother nature is adverse. For more details on benign and adverse strategies, see References 2 and 6.

4.7. HANDLING IRREDUCIBLES

No attempt should be made to reduce all the data and information to numbers and analytical approaches. Many aspects are inherently nonquantifiable, or *irreducible*, e.g., customer satisfaction, environmental impacts, and social concerns. These kinds of aspects should be left unquantified. The focus should be on quantifying and reducing aspects which are most readily and most appropriately quantified. This will effectively reduce the amount of intuition required, and facilitate the management decision making process. Judgment and intuition will still be required with regard to the remaining irreducibles.

4.8. SUMMARY AND CONCLUSIONS

This chapter has presented and discussed various techniques for collecting, assembling, and reducing appraisal data. The proper use of these techniques is an important part of the preparation for project appraisals and project selection decision making.

The use of the techniques in this chapter can increase the effectiveness of the appraisal and selection process in three important ways. First, these techniques can assist in reducing and collating large amounts of various data into an overall, consistent picture. Second, the techniques can help to quantify and measure the relative cost, value, risk and suitability of each of the candidate proposals. Third, the techniques will provide a better distinction between those aspects that are amenable to analytical treatment and the irreducibles which must be reckoned with intuitively and judgmentally.

4.9. REFERENCES

1. Souder, W. E. "Project Planning and Control," Chapter 10 of *The Handbook of Operations Research*. New York: Van Nostrand Reinhold, 1978, pp. 301–344.
2. Souder, W. E. *Management Decision Methods for Managers of Engineering and Research*. New York: Van Nostrand Reinhold, 1980, pp. 36–78.
3. Rowe, W. *An Anatomy of Risk*. New York: John Wiley and Sons, 1978.
4. Miles, L. D. *Techniques of Value Analysis and Engineering*. New York: McGraw-Hill, 1972.
5. Canada, J. R. *Intermediate Economic Analysis for Management and Engineering*. New Jersey: Prentice-Hall, 1971, pp. 171–392.
6. Fishburn, Peter C. *Decision and Value Theory*. New York: Wiley, 1964, pp. 18–242.

5. Appraisal and Selection of Ideas and Proposals

5.0. IDEA FLOW AND PROJECT SELECTION

As discussed in Chapter 1, the term "project selection" encompasses several different decision processes. It may involve the choice of the one best project. Or it may refer to the screening out of unacceptable proposals. It may also involve the choice of the best allocation of a budget among a portfolio of projects.

Figure 5.1 details the idea flow process and the associated types of project selection decision problems that are often encountered in many organizations. Typically, new product ideas and project proposals continuously arrive from many different sources, e.g., employees, customers and suppliers. The subsequent processing and disposition of these new product and project ideas often involves many different types of analyses and evaluations, as illustrated in Figure 5.1.

In screening, the idea is analyzed in a preliminary fashion, on the basis of its most prominent criteria or characteristics. The screening process is a kind of quick and inexpensive first level analysis of the idea. The results from the screening process may suggest that the idea should be rejected because it is not meritorious ("Abandon idea" in Figure 5.1). Or the idea may be temporarily backlogged ("Idea backlog") in deference to a higher priority idea. Or the idea may be deemed so urgent ("Urgent item") or so obviously beneficial to the organization that it is accorded priority over all other efforts. Alternatively, the results of the screening analysis may indicate that the idea warrants further investigation and a more in-depth analysis.

In a more in-depth analysis, the idea proposal will be subjected to an evaluation process (Figure 5.1). In this process, a much more

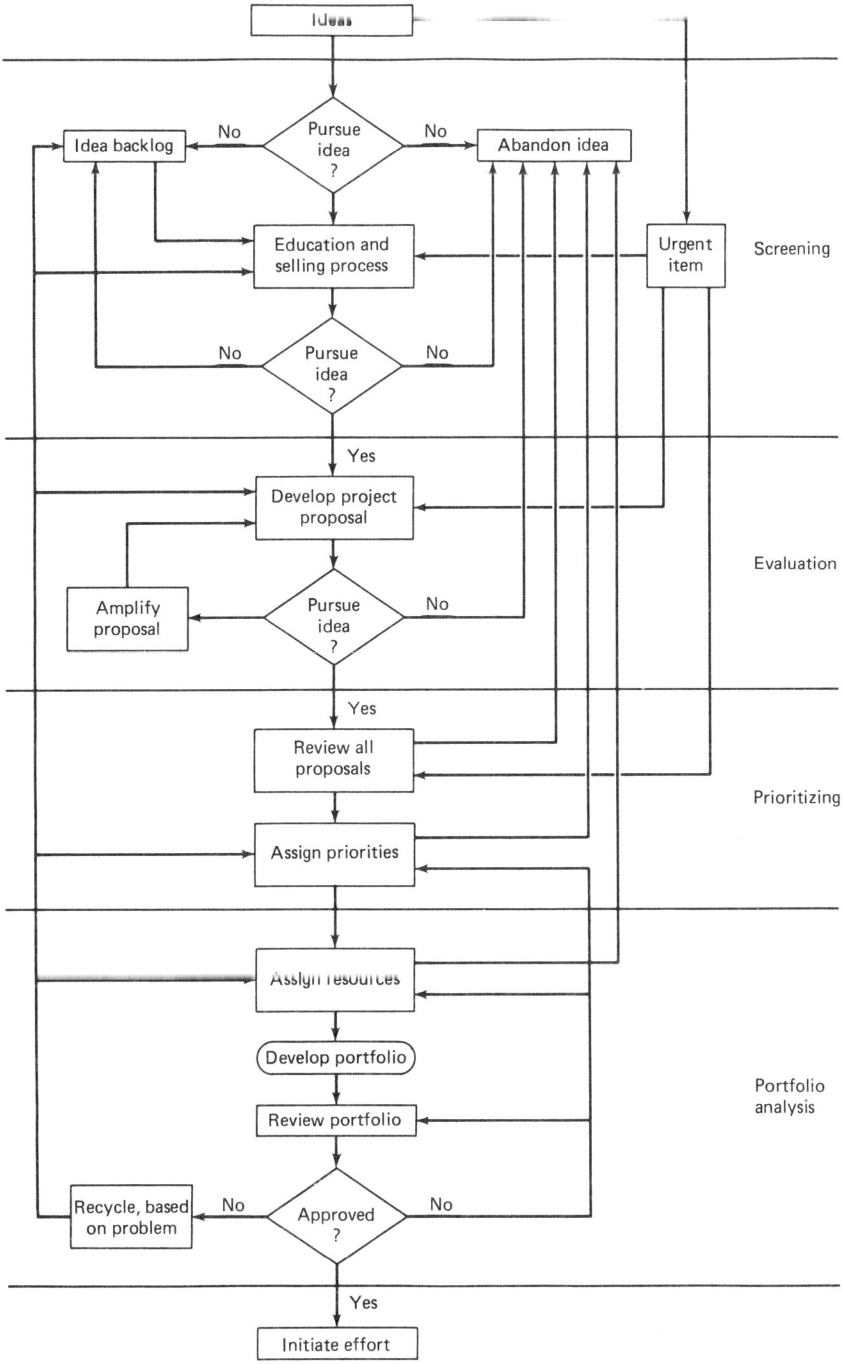

Figure 5.1. A project selection process.

rigorous, in-depth and comprehensive analysis will be made of the characteristics and potentials of the proposal. As with the screening process, the evaluation process may result in several dispositions of the proposal. It may be rejected and abandoned for lack of meritorious characteristics. Or it may be backlogged for later retrieval and analyses. Or it may be found to be meritorious and acceptable. The results may indicate that the idea is so meritorious that work on it should be initiated immediately ("Urgent item").

The results from the evaluation process may indicate that the proposal should be competitively assessed and prioritized against all the other ideas. In a prioritizing process, the relative strengths and weaknesses of the candidates are carefully appraised. A prioritized ranking of all the candidates is sought on the basis of these appraisals.

The decision to fund an idea and initiate work on it involves a consideration of the available human and financial resources. The level of available funds and personnel skill types, and the commitments to the ongoing portfolio of efforts must be considered. It may be that the new idea is so meritorious that it should replace one or more of the ongoing project efforts. If this is the case, then some ongoing project will be terminated or temporarily halted while resources are allocated to the new idea and work on it then proceeds. Portfolio analysis models have been developed to aid in making these comparisons and analyses. A portfolio model determines the best way to allocate the available budget among all the alternative projects, including the new candidates and the ongoing portfolio of funded projects.

5.1. DYNAMICS OF PROJECT SELECTION

As Figure 5.1 suggests, project selection decision making can be a very dynamic process. Screening, evaluation, prioritizing, and portfolio analysis decisions may be made at various points, and a new idea may not even go through these processes in sequence. An idea may be backlogged or abandoned at several points. Backlogged projects will usually be retrieved at some later point in time, whereas abandoned projects will usually not be. On the other hand, new information and changed circumstances may make a previously rejected (abandoned) project suddenly more attractive. Or new information and changed circumstances may cause a previously back-logged project to be rejected.

The available budget or manpower skill types may constrain the project selection process. If the budget is inadequate to fund a particular project which appears meritorious, that project may then be backlogged for lack of resources. Alternatively, the project may be divisible, in that certain portions of it may be performed or work on some portions of the project can be initiated, while the remaining portions of the project are backlogged.

Customer complaints, competitive threats, or unique opportunities may result in an urgent item that takes priority over other ideas. Depending on the urgency, the urgent item may only receive a cursory screening and evaluation, and it may go directly to the portfolio decision stage.

Screening, evaluation, prioritizing, and portfolio decisions may be repeated several times over the life cycle of a project, in response to emerging new ideas and changing circumstances. The advent of a new idea, a change in competitive pressures, or the appearance of a new technology are examples of changes that may cause management to reevaluate a previously selected project. Moreover, with each achievement that is made on the ongoing projects, new technical information will be forthcoming that may impact on other efforts and proposed ideas. As the ongoing project efforts come nearer to their completion, key personnel and equipment may be released that can be used on another proposed idea, perhaps one that was previously backlogged for lack of resources.

5.2. BEHAVIORAL ASPECTS

Many different individuals throughout the organization will normally become involved in the evaluation and selection of new product ideas and project proposals. Information will usually be supplied to the evaluation process by research, engineering, marketing, planning, financial and production personnel. Thus, problems in information collection and information sharing, and differences in viewpoints and perspectives may come into play.

The choice of one idea over another will usually impact several departments within the organization. The talents and resources of several departments, e.g., engineering, marketing, research, and production, will be required to successfully perform and complete the project work. Thus, if some departments are unwilling (or unable) to support the proposed idea, it may be rejected and abandoned for that reason alone. In general, the choice of one idea over another is likely to be heavily influenced by the emotional commitments, loyalties and power patterns within an organization.

5.3. ANALYTICAL AND BEHAVIORAL DECISION AIDS

The evaluation and selection of new product ideas and project proposals is thus a complex process, consisting of many interrelated decision subprocesses. The complexities involve the varieties of information that must be collected, and the difficulty of unequivocally measuring and assessing candidate projects on the basis of this information. Much of the information is subjective and uncertain in nature. Many of the ideas and proposals exist as embryonic thoughts that are propelled by the sponsor's enthusiasm. Selecting the best idea is often further complicated by the presence of various organization-behavior factors that tend to politicize the decision making.

Several analytical and behavioral decision making aids have been developed. These include screening and evaluation methods, prioritizing and portfolio models, and group decision process methods.

5.4. SCREENING METHODS

Screening methods are quick and easy to use. They are appropriate for eliminating the most undesirable proposals from further consideration. Because they require a relatively small amount of information, they can be used where the available data are limited or only rough estimates are possible. On the other hand, screening models do not provide a great depth of analysis, and they should be used accordingly.

5.4.1. Profiles

Table 5.1 presents an illustration of the application of a profile. To develop a profile, a list of criteria or requirements is first set forth. Then the extent to which each of the candidate ideas or proposed projects meet these criteria or requirements is rated as either

Table 5.1. Illustration of A Profile for Two Project. A and B.

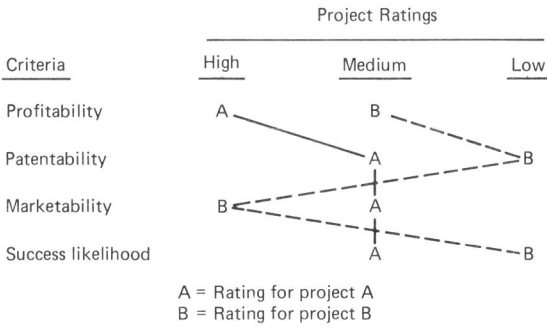

	Project Ratings		
Criteria	High	Medium	Low
Profitability	A	B	
Patentability		A	B
Marketability	B	A	
Success likelihood		A	B

A = Rating for project A
B = Rating for project B

high, medium, or low. Note that no numbers are used. Instead, the proposals or projects are compared on the basis of a subjective evaluation of their characteristics or attributes. The ratings can be done by a committee or by a single individual. Or the profiles developed by two or more individuals can be compared. For example, marketing and research personnel could compare their independently derived profiles.

The advantage of a profile model lies in its simplicity and ease of use. The outputs from a profile model are easily communicated to others, and they provide a pictorial display of the project's merits and limitations. For example, in Table 5.1, it is obvious at a glance that project A is generally a medium to high performer, superior to project B on all of the criteria but one.

On the other hand, this illustration shows that profiles have some inherent limitations. This type of analysis does not tell us anything about the tradeoffs among the criteria. For example, the profile doesn't tell us whether the high performance of project B on the marketability criterion compensates in any way for its medium and low performances on the other criteria. Thus, profile models are really starting points for other analyses. They are best used as stimulants to further inquiry and dialogue.

Though the choice of criteria and rating descriptors ("high," "medium," etc.) for a profile is normally not a difficult problem, efforts should be made to make sure all the parties agree on the meaning and the use of these choices in designing the profile. The descriptors should be sufficiently well-defined that all the involved parties understand them, and the criteria should be ones that everyone feels are relevant for judging the candidate projects.

Table 5.2. Illustration of a Scaling Model for One Project, Project A.

	Criteria	−2	−1	0	+1	+2
Top management	Capital requirements					X
	Competitive reaction				X	
	Return on investment				X	
	Payout time	■			X	■
	Wall Street impacts				X	
Engineering	Required equipment					X
	Availability of personnel					X
	Know-how					X
	Design difficulty	■	■	■		
	Equipment availability				X	
	Piping layouts				X	
Research	Patentability			X		
	Likelihood of success					X
	Know-how					X
	Project costs		X			
	Availability of personnel	X				
	Availability of laboratory	X				
Marketing	Length of product life		X			
	Product advantage	■	X	■		■
	Suitability to salesforce	X				
	Size of market	X				
	Number of competitors	X				
Production	Processability					X
	Know-how					X
	Equipment availability					X
	Number of X's	5	3	2	7	7

Key: +2 = Excellent
+1 = Good
0 = Fair
−1 = Bad
−2 = Unacceptable

■ = Not applicable
⊠ = Score for project A

5.4.2. Scaling Models

Like a profile, a scaling model consists of a list of criteria. Usually, this list is quite comprehensive. A scoring scale is then developed and applied to obtain numerical ratings. An illustration is shown in Table 5.2.

The resulting visual display of X's communicates the various strengths and weaknesses of the project, and the summary number of X's at the bottom of the chart adds to the analysis. The clustering of the criteria into areas of concern for top management, engineering, etc. provides an opportunity for each of these parties to rate the project and supply the X's for their areas. The completed chart can then serve as a focus for communication and discussion among the parties, as an aid to the final decision to accept or reject the project. For example, as Table 5.2 shows, project A's major weaknesses are in the marketing area. However, the research pesonnel also perceive that project A is unacceptable in some important regards. These perceptions need to be thoroughly discussed, and the project's potentials should be more thoroughly probed and investigated with respect to these bad and unacceptable areas.

Word scales (Excellent, etc.) could be used in lieu of a numerical scale (-2, -1, etc.), though numerical scales generally have greater visual impact. However, there is some danger that a numerical scale may give the impression that the ratings are more quantitative than they actually are. Note from Table 5.2 how a scaling model permits the mixing of 3-point scales ("Payout time"), 2-point scales ("Product advantage") and 5-point scales (all the other criteria). This is a decided advantage in those cases where some criteria are naturally dichotomous (i.e., either good or bad) or trichotomous (i.e., either good, fair, or bad).

An extensive list of criteria and scales for a scaling model can usually be developed through a series of group sessions. Creativity methods may be used to assist in these sessions (see Chapter 3), as well as other group decision making methods [1, 2, 3]. It is important for all the involved parties to come to consensus agreement and understanding on the list of criteria and the scales.

Table 5.3. Illustration of a Checklist for Three Projects.

Projects	Profitability			Marketability			Success likelihood			Total score
	3	2	1	3	2	1	3	2	1	
Project A	✓			✓			✓			7
Project B		✓		✓					✓	6
Project C			✓			✓			✓	3

Criteria

5.4.3. Checklists

Table 5.3 presents an example of a checklist. Like a profile, each candidate project or proposal is subjectively evaluated and scored. Like a scaling model, numerical scales are used. But in a checklist, an overall numerical score is derived for each evaluated project. The total score for each project is simply the sum of the scores on each criterion. Checklists thus provide both a graphic profile of checkmarks and also a total numerical score for each project.

Thus, checklists combine many of the advantages of both a profile and a scaling model. The total scores provide a more accurate picture of the target achievements of the various projects, and they facilitate a comparison of several candidate projects.

In general, profiles, scaling models and checklists have been extensively applied throughout the chemical and pharmaceuticals industries. For examples the reader should consult References 3, 4, 5, and 6.

5.5. EVALUATION METHODS

Relative to screening methods, evaluation methods provide a much more detailed and in-depth analysis, permitting finer discriminations among candidate projects. On the other hand, while they provide a more comprehensive and accurate analysis, they also require a much

Table 5.4. Illustration of A Scoring Model.

Criteria	Profitability	Patentability	Marketability	Produceability
Criterion weights	4	3	2	1

Projects	Criterion scores*				Total weighted score
Project D	10	6	4	3	69
Project E	5	10	10	5	75
Project F	3	7	10	10	63

Total weighted score$_i$ = Σ_j Criterion score$_{ij}$ × Criterion weight$_j$

*Scale: 10 = Excellent; 1 = Unacceptable

greater detail of input data. However, it is difficult to make a project selection decision without the kind of information that goes into an evaluation method.

5.5.1. Scoring Models

Table 5.4 shows an example of a scoring model and indicates how such a model can be applied. Each candidate project is scored on each criterion, using an appropriate scoring scale. This results in a set of criterion scores. Each criterion is weighted relative to its perceived importance, resulting in a set of criterion weights. These scores and weights are combined according to the following model:

$$T_i = \sum_j s_{ij} \times w_j. \tag{5.1}$$

Here, T_i is the total weighted score for project i, s_{ij} is the criterion score for the ith project on the jth criterion, and w_j is the criterion weight for the jth criterion.

The advantage of a scoring model is that it takes into account the tradeoffs among the criteria, as defined by the criterion weights. For example, the unweighted total score for project E is 5 + 10 +

$10 + 5 = 30$ and the unweighted total score for project F is $3 + 7 + 10 + 10 = 30$. Since both projects have the same total score, are they therefore equivalent? The results from the scoring model tell us otherwise: Project E is superior to Project F. The criterion weights, which specify the relative importance of the criteria, denote that profitability and patentability are the more important criteria. Since Project E scores higher than project F on these two important criteria, its total weighted score is necessarily larger.

Developing appropriate weighting factors is thus essential in the construction of a valid scoring model. Though more sophisticated techniques are available [3, 7, 8], suitable weights can usually be developed through a group rating/ranking exercise. The choice of group members will depend on the intended use of the scoring model. For example, if the scoring model is to be used for rating exploratory research projects, then exploratory research personnel should be adequately represented in the group. The rating/ranking exercises themselves can be highly informative, as well as useful communication and team building experiences [1, 2, 3].

5.5.2. Goal Contribution Models

Goal contribution models permit the decision maker to evaluate projects with regard to the degree of contribution which they make to the organizational goals. An example of an application of a goal contribution model is shown in Table 5.5.

To develop a goal contribution model, first list the hierarchy of goals. In the example shown in Table 5.5, the hierarchy consists of short range goals and long range supergoals. The short range goals include concerns for profitability, marketability, and energy savings. The long range supergoals consist of only two concerns: technological and market supremacy. This hierarchy of goals is then value-weighted according to the degree to which management feels that each goal is important to the overall objectives of the company. Though more sophisticated techniques exist [3, 10], the value-weighting can be accomplished by allocating a given number of points among the goals in such a way that the point-allocations reflect their relative values. For example, in Table 5.5, a total of 100 points has been allocated 70/30 to the short range and long range supergoals, respectively. This indicates that, collectively, the

Table 5.5. Example of A Goal Contribution Model.

PROJECT RATINGS*

| | SHORT RANGE OPERATING EFFICIENCY ($V = 70$) | | | LONG RANGE DOMINANCE ($V = 30$) | | |
	PROFITABILITY ($V = 30$)	MARKETABILITY ($V = 25$)	ENERGY SAVINGS ($V = 15$)	TECHNOLOGICAL SUPREMACY ($V = 20$)	MARKET SUPREMACY ($V = 10$)	TOTAL GOAL CONTRIBUTION
Project H	25	20	15	5	5	70
Project J	15	10	5	20	10	60
Project K	30	20	0	20	5	75

* V = value weight; the importance of that goal to company objectives; the contribution that a superior project would make to that goal.

short range concerns are viewed as more than twice as important as the long range concerns. The 70 points are then allocated among the three short range subgoals according to their perceived value. And the remaining 30 points are similarly allocated among the long range supergoals. The complete set of value-weights thus indicates the perfect levels of contribution which the ideal project could make. For instance, in Table 5.5, a perfect project would score 30 on profitability, 25 on marketability, etc. Thus, a perfect project would have a total goal contribution score of 100 points.

In the application shown in Table 5.5, it is obvious that project H is short range oriented, project J is long range oriented, and project K is a combination of orientations. Note that project K is less than perfect on most of the goals. However, project K's high scores on the high-value profitability, marketability, and technological supremacy goals sum to a high total goal contribution for project K.

The advantage of a goal contribution model is that it permits the decision maker to think in terms of the goals of the candidate projects and the levels of goal achievement within the organization. Thus, goal contribution models may be especially useful when the decision maker is attempting to assemble a balanced portfolio of several projects. For example, as shown in Table 5.5, projects H and J taken together provide major contributions to the long range goals and major contributions to each of the short range goals.

5.6. PRIORITIZING MODELS

Few organizations have enough resources to work on all their good ideas at the same time. Moreover, some ideas will be better than others, some will be inferior to others, and some will be more urgent than others. Thus, the need often arises to rank or prioritize ideas and project proposals according to some measures of their "goodness." Prioritizing models are designed to fill this need.

5.6.1. Economic Index Models

One commonly used economic index model is the return on investment (ROI) index:

$$\text{ROI index} = P^*/I^*, \qquad (5.2)$$

where $P^* = \sum_i P_i/(1 + r)^i$ and $I^* = \sum_i I_i/(1 + r)^i$. Here P_i is the anticipated dollar profit from the project in the ith year, I_i is the total investment made in the ith year of the project's life, and r is an interest rate. The quantities P^* and I^* are the total discounted present values of all the P_i and I_i numbers. Candidate projects may be prioritized on the basis of their ROI indexes.

A large variety of index models have been developed [3, 11, 12, 13]. They all have the general form

$$I = R/C \qquad (5.3)$$

where I is the index. An example is Olsen's Index [13], where $R = r \times d \times p \times s \times q \times n$ and C is the total project cost. Here, r is the probability of research success, d is the probability of development success, p is the probability of market success, s is the annual dollar sales from the product if the project succeeds, q is the percent profit, and n is the number of years of market life of the product. Another example is Viller's Index [13], where $R = r \times d \times p(E - D)$. Here, E is the present value of all future earnings from the project and D is the present worth cost of all the research and development activities.

An illustration of the use of an index model is shown in Table 5.6. The project priorities are based on a ranking of the projects according to their ROI indexes. This type of prioritizing analysis often provides a starting point for dialogs and other analyses. For example, the data in Table 5.6 raise a question as to whether work should be initiated on the low-investment project M or the high-investment project X or both. If the organization has limited funds, then top management may choose the low-investment project M over project X. On the other hand, project X may be more appealing to the sales manager because

Table 5.6. Illustration of An Application of an Index Model.

	P^*	I^*	ROI INDEX	PRIORITY
Project X	$1,000,000	$8,197	122	1st
Project M	500,000	4,132	121	2nd
Project Z	750,000	9,036	83	3rd
Project L	500,000	10,000	50	4th
Project T	360,000	9,230	39	5th

of its larger dollar potential. Note that project M may be viewed as less risky, in the sense that less money is invested, so there is less money to be lost if the project does not succeed.

5.6.2. Figure of Merit Models

Figure of merit models are analogous to economic index models, in that the output from the model is an index number that can be used to rank or prioritize candidate projects. However, a figure of merit model does not use any economic inputs. An example is

$$\text{Figure of merit} = r \times d \times p(T + M), \qquad (5.4)$$

where T and M are ratings of the technical and market merits of the project, and r, d, and p are probabilities, as defined above. The T and M variables can be subjective assessments, the outputs from a scoring model, etc.

Another example is

$$\text{Research figure of merit} = (1 - r)(1 - p)\frac{\text{AR} - I}{C}, \qquad (5.5)$$

where AR is the anticipated regrets if the project is not undertaken, and C is the cost to complete the research and development on the project. Here, AR may be the lost sales, the foregone profits, etc., if the project is not undertaken. The other symbols are as defined above. A large number of figure of merit models have been developed [3, 13].

5.7. PORTFOLIO AND BUDGET ALLOCATION MODELS

When the objective is to determine the best allocation of funds among several projects, portfolio models are called for. An example of a portfolio problem is presented in Table 5.7. In this situation, a total of $300,000 is available for selecting and funding one or two of the three projects, at one of their three alternative funding levels. The expected profits vary with the project funding levels. This is because the higher project funding levels result in more advanced products, which will achieve a larger market share. What is the best allocation of the available funds? Which projects should be selected? At what levels should they be funded?

The answers to these questions are: select and fund project C at the $200,000 level, and select and fund project B at $100,000 level, and reject project A. The available funds will be used up and the total expected profits will be $450M + $275M = $725M. There is no better allocation of the $300,000. This is the optimum allocation: it gives the largest total expected profits.

It is interesting to note what would happen if only $200,000 were available. In that case, the optimum portfolio would consist of only project C, funded at $200,000. Project A and project B should be rejected. There would not be enough money to fund any other projects. Note that an alternative portfolio allocation is to fund both project A and project B at $100,000 each and to reject project C. But this would yield total expected profits of $100M + $275M = $375M, which is $75M less than the total expected profits for allocating all the money to project C.

Note that if $400,000 is available, then the optimum portfolio is to select and fund both project C and project A at $200,000 each, and to reject project B. This allocation yields the largest total expected profits: $450M + $350M = $800M. Recall that the portfolio was restricted to no more than two projects (due to personnel limits). Otherwise, all three projects could be selected here.

5.7.1. Types of Portfolio Models

In the simple illustration in Table 5.7, the optimum portfolio can be obtained by inspection and trial and error. But when there are many

Table 5.7. Example of a Portfolio Problem.

AVAILABLE FUNDS = $300,000			
ALTERNATIVE FUNDING LEVELS FOR EACH PROJECT	EXPECTED PROFITS CORRESPONDING TO EACH FUNDING LEVEL, IN $M		
	PROJECT A	PROJECT B	PROJECT C
$ 0	$ 0	$ 0	$ 0
100,000	100	275	15
200,000	350	300	450

projects, then mathematical algorithms and computer programs can enormously facilitate the choice of the optimum portfolio. The type of algorithm used will depend on the nature of the decision problem. The following three cases are possible.

If the projects are mutually exclusive, then each project can be funded at one and only one level. This case is illustrated in Table 5.7. An algorithm is given for this case in Chapter 7 (Table 7.1) where its application is illustrated for capital investment projects. The algorithm is a general one, and it can be applied to any types of projects—capital investment projects, research projects, development projects, engineering projects, personal investments, etc.

If the projects are not mutually exclusive, then several different versions of the same project may be selected. For instance, if the projects in Table 5.7 had not been mutually exclusive, then for the $300,000 budget one of the alternatives would be to select or purchase three project A's at $100,000 each. Another alternative would be to purchase three project B's at $100,000 each, etc. The optimum portfolio for a $300,000 budget would then simply be to purchase three project B's. The procedures for this type of portfolio problem are also given in Chapter 7 (Section 7.3.1).

Finally, the projects may be "zero-one" in nature. That is, each project can either be rejected (zero-funded), or selected and funded at only one funding level (one-funded). To illustrate, let us examine the data in Table 5.8. If the budget is $200,000, then the only way to spend the budget is to fund project B at its only level, $200,000 for a total expected profit of $300M. For a $300,000 budget, the optimum portfolio is project A plus project B, yielding total expected profits of $400M. For a $150,000 budget, the optimum portfolio consists of only project A—and $50,000 is unspent. The algorithm for this case is also detailed in Chapter 7 (Table 7.5). It, too, is a general one.

Table 5.8. The Zero-One Case.

ALTERNATIVE FUNDING LEVELS	EXPECTED PROFITS CORRESPONDING TO EACH FUNDING LEVEL, IN $M		
	PROJECT A	PROJECT B	PROJECT C
$ 0	$ 0	$ 0	$ 0
100,000	100	—	15
200,000	—	300	—

A large number of portfolio models have been developed [3, 11, 13, 14, 15]. The models differ in terms of the types of input data used, the nature of the decision problem (mutually exclusive projects, etc.), what the decision maker wishes to maximize (profits, sales, etc.), the riskiness of the situation, and other aspects. In general, the portfolio problem may be represented mathematically as follows:

$$\text{Maximize:} \quad Z = p \times f(x_j) \quad (5.6)$$

$$\text{Subject to:} \quad g_i(x_j) \le b_i \quad (5.7)$$

$$c_i x_j \le B, \quad (5.8)$$

where $f(x_j)$ is the objective function, e.g., maximize profits, p is a parameter for risk, $0 \le p \le 1$, $g_i(x_j) = b_i$ is a set of resource constraints, c_i is a unit resource cost, and B is a dollar budget. Linear, nonlinear, and other mathematical programming techniques are thus often used to find solutions to portfolio problems [3, 16].

5.7.2. Selecting the Optimum Budget

Let us now return to the data in Table 5.7. Using these data, Figure 5.2 displays the optimum portfolios and their associated total expected profits, for four alternative budgets. Note how the rate of increase in the total expected profit—denoted as Δ in Figure 5.2—first increases and then decreases, as the budget increases from $100,000 to $400,000. This is a typical pattern. The reasons for this pattern are easy to deduce. Succinctly, the smaller budgets are overly constraining, and do not permit the best project funding level combinations to be selected. On the other hand, by the time the larger budgets are reached, the best project-funding combinations have already been selected. Thus, there is often an optimum sized budget, somewhere between the largest and smallest alternative budgets.

More information is needed in order to determine the optimum sized budget for the situation depicted in Figure 5.2. However, the principle is easily illustrated as follows. Suppose that, faced with the situation depicted in Figure 5.2, the firm can always invest $100,000 in a new business venture that will pay back $76M. Then they should not set a budget of more than $300,000 for the portfolio problem

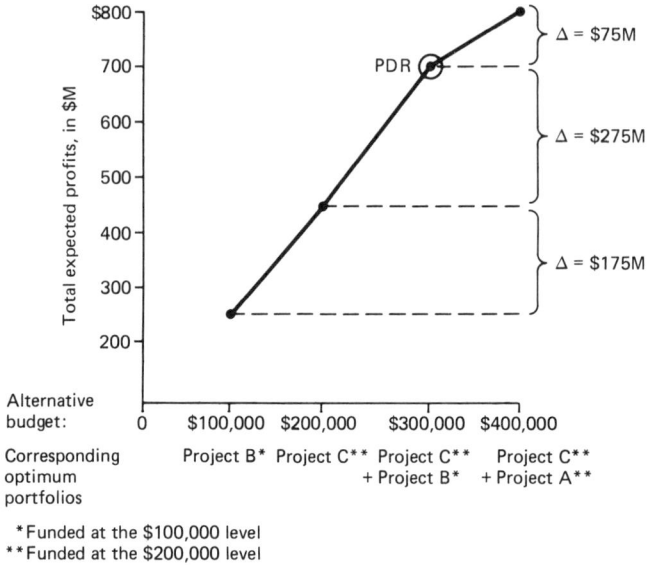

Figure 5.2. Portfolio budgets.

depicted here. Any excess funds beyond $300,000 should be invested in the new business venture, where it will return $760 per $1 invested. Investing more than $300,000 in the projects will only return $750 per $1 invested. The $300,000 budget is the point of diminishing returns (PDR).

5.8. GROUP DECISION PROCESS METHODS[1]

Most project selection decision data are necessarily subjective in nature. Unless a spirit of trust and openness is felt by the parties, it is not likely that such data will be fully and openly exchanged. Each person who is involved, either as a project proposer, a decider, or a supplier of information, must appreciate the larger needs of the organization vis-à-vis his own. Ideally, all parties should be able to comprehend, empathize and come to consensus with each other. The involved parties must understand and truly comprehend the

---

[1] Portions of the material in this section are reprinted from W. E. Souder, "A System for Using R&D Project Evaluation Methods," *Research Management*, Vol. 21, No. 5, September 1978, pp. 29–37, by permission.

nature of the projects they are proposing or deliberating. This means two things. It means they must have a depth of factual knowledge. And it also means that they must have an objective sense of their own feelings, since much of the decision data are highly personal. Many decision settings fail because the participant's feelings are not crystallized, and the parties literally do not know how they feel about a particular project. One process that effectively fulfills many of these needs is the QS/NI decision process [3, 9, 10].

5.8.1. The QS/NI Decision Process

This process combines the use of psychometric methods and controlled group interactions. Though a variety of psychometric methods may be used, the Q-sort (QS) method has been found to be the simplest

RESULT AT EACH STEP

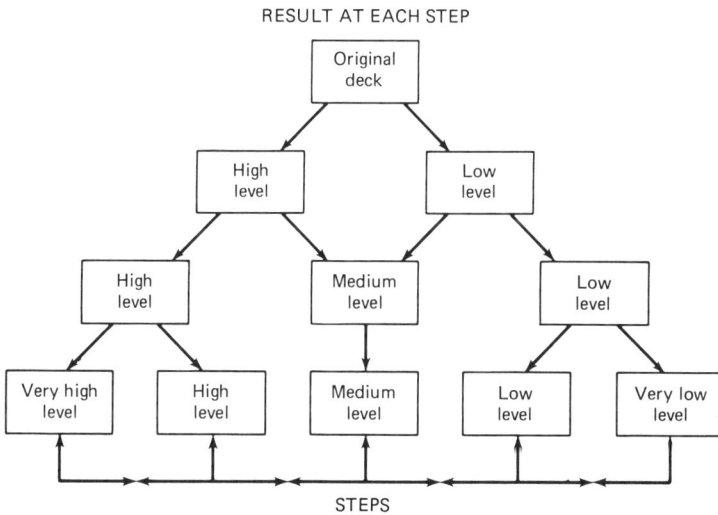

STEPS

1. An individual is given a stack of cards, each card bearing the name, title or number of one project. The individual is asked to perform the following sorting operations. A specified criterion (e.g., "priority") is the basis for sorting.
2. Divide the deck into two piles, one representing a high level of the specified criterion, the other a low level. (The piles need not be equal.)
3. Select cards from each pile to form a third pile representing the medium level of the criterion.
4. Select cards from the high level pile to yield another pile representing the very high level of the criterion; select cards from the low level pile to yield another pile representing the very low level of the criterion.
5. Finally, survey the selections and shift any cards that seem out of place until the classifications are satisfactory.

Figure 5.3. Mechanics of a Q-Sort.

and the most effective for rank-order classifying a population of R&D projects [3]. The mechanics of this method are relatively simple, as outlined in Figure 5.3. An individual is given a deck of cards, with each card bearing the name and identification of one of the projects. He then successively sorts and re-sorts the deck of cards into five predesignated categories, according to predefined criteria or priorities. As a result, the population of projects is arrayed into five priority categories. These procedures are described in more detail elsewhere [3, 9, 10].

The nominal-interacting (NI) process begins with a nominal period in which each individual in the group silently and anonymously completes a Q-sort exercise on the population of projects to be evaluated. These individual Q-sort results are then tabulated in a tally chart, which is displayed to the entire group with an overhead projector. (Table 5.9 presents an example of a tally chart, which is discussed below.) This chart focuses on the group agreement/disagreement statistics, while preserving individual anonymity. The group is then given a period in which they can interact and discuss the results. In this interacting period, the discussions are fully controlled by the participants. They may share opinions, exchange data, challenge each other, negotiate, remain placid, etc. The anonymity of the tally charts permits members to take the easy choice of not responding to threatening or vituperative questions about who voted for what. Minority opinions may thus be preserved because they are not subject to specious group persuasion. Experience shows that the unstructuredness of the group permits the underlying sociometry and influence centers to emerge naturally, so that the group may work out its own opinion modification and accommodation patterns. To help guide these accommodation patterns, the group's effectiveness and team building tendencies (e.g., hedonic tone, potency, trust, cohesiveness, etc.) can be periodically measured and fed back to the group [1, 2, 3, 9, 10].

This sequence of an individual Q-sort period (the nominal period) and a group discussion period (the interacting period) can be repeated for several rounds. Experience shows that two to three rounds are needed to stimulate complete information exchange, but more than four rounds dissipates the subjects [1, 3, 9]. The first nominal period permits individuals to document their own thoughts and value judgments. The first interacting period confronts the group with a diversity of opinions to be resolved. The second nominal period permits each individual to privately restructure their thoughts. The second intelacting period provides an opportunity to refine opinions and work toward consensus. A third nominal period provides the environment for closure and consensus. A consensus will usually emerge as the members adopt ideas and opinions from each other, acquire more information and interpersonal understanding, or become influenced by the enthusiasm of the group. The tally chart itself is consensus-inducing, for those members who identify with the group. The feelings of group identity, the loyalties, and the partnerships developed during the QS/NI exercises are also very important. Experience shows that they can be vital for future organization decision making [1, 2].

Table 5.9 provides an actual example of a tally chart for 20 subjects and 13 projects, at the end of two nominal and one interacting periods. The arrows trace the changes in the individual Q-sorts from the first to the second nominal period. Note that the degree of consensus actually declined during this part of the exercise for projects C, H, and K. In this case, the discussions revealed a heretofore hidden lack of information and a fundamental lack of comprehension of these projects by some of the subjects. These three proposals were returned to the submitters for additional work and subsequent re-submittal. A consensus was reached on these resubmitted projects at the end of another round of the QS/NI process.

The Q-sorts and the intense discussions fequently reveal hidden gaps in information and comprehensions, and point the way to their elimination. The QS/NI process also usually reveals a great deal about group interaction patterns and interpersonal power play strategies. Coalitions, and advocate and adversary positions, are usually made very visible by the QS/NI process [3, 2].

5.8.2. Goals and Criteria

One of the essential prerequisites to any project selection system is a set of clearly defined and agreed-upon organizational goals and project selection criteria. Goals and criteria are the ultimate standards for killing some projects and accepting others. Parties who agree to the goals will necessarily also understand what types of projects are acceptable and how their proposals will be judged.

The QS/NI process has been found to be very helpful in establishing a consensus set of goals and project selection critera [1, 2, 3]. The

Table 5.9. Example of a Tally Chart.

Tally chart for 20 subjects and 13 projects at the end of the following sequence of periods: Nominal-Interacting-Nominal. Projects evidencing consensus at the end of the second nominal period = A, B, D, E, F, G, I, J, L, M. All projects evidenced consensus at the end of an additional subsequent interacting-nominal sequence. Consensus is measured by standard statistical tests and the subject's feelings. For more details see References 3 and 10.

Q-sorting method provides the analytical structure for rating and ranking the goals. The NI process provides a climate that is conducive to the generation of ideas and suggestions for goal statements and objectives. Moreover, the process provides a framework for the effective achievement of group consensus and commitment to those goals. The resulting consensus and group climate appear to provide many long-lasting organizational benefits in terms of interdepartmental collaboration and joint cooperation [1, 2].

5.9. SUMMARY: A PROJECT SELECTION SYSTEM

Once a consensus set of goals is established, various project selection methods and models can be used in combination with the NI process. As outlined in Figure 5.4, different models can be substituted for the Q-sorting exercise in the QS/NI process, depending on the type of evaluation problem and the types of projects being assessed. The project selection model satisfies the need for an analytical aid, and the NI process assists in fulfilling the organization behavioral needs. For example, with exploratory projects, the evaluation data are often highly subjective and meager. Therefore, screening methods are ap-

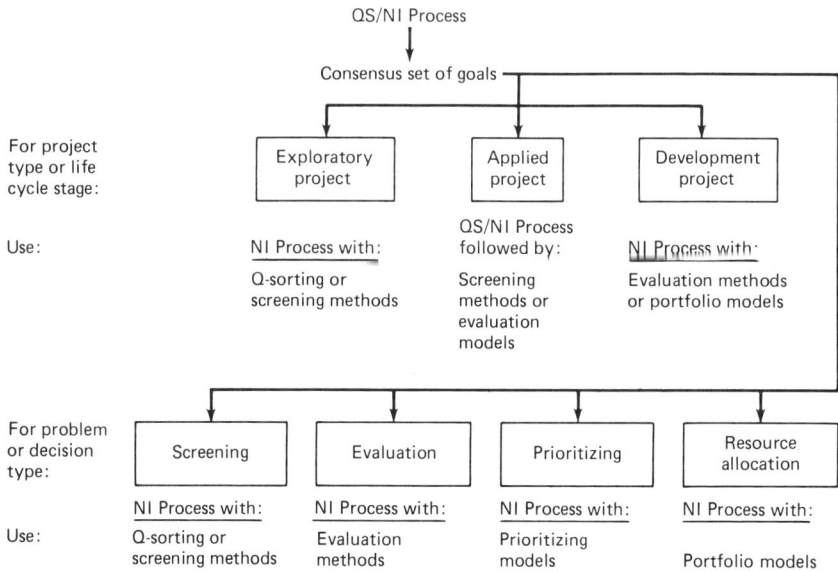

Figure 5.4. A project selection and evaluation system.

propriate because they require a minimum of data. The NI process is also appropriate because it handles the subjective evaluation and opinion exchange process.

In the case of applied research projects, the evaluation data will usually be relatively less subjective and more plentiful. Thus, evaluation methods are appropriate. However, it seems reasonable to use Q-sorting first as a screening device, and then to follow it up with an evaluation method for detailed project discriminations. For instance, an evaluation method could be applied to each project that has been Q-sorted into the same priority category, in order to develop a unique priority for each project. This combination of the QS/NI process as a preliminary screen and an evaluation method as a final screening can provide efficiency and effectiveness to the entire process.

In the case of development projects, the amount and quality of data available on each project may be sufficient for the use of sophisticated computerized portfolio models. For instance, the input data for a computerized model could be solicited in a nominal setting. The outputs from the computer model could then be discussed and analyzed in an interacting setting, followed by another nominal setting of data solicitation, and a subsequent computer run. This sequence could be repeated until a satisfactory decision was achieved. This process has in fact been successfully used in one organization, and the experiences are reported in the literature [17]. Of course, any of the less-sophisticated models (Q-sorting, etc.) could also be used on development projects.

As Figure 5.4 shows, the nature of the decision problem may also govern the choice of project selection methods and models used. For screening decisions, only "ballpark" accept/reject evaluations of projects are needed. A combination of the NI process and Q-sorting or screening methods is ideal here. By comparison, project prioritizing and resource allocation decisions usually involve projects whose attributes are relatively better understood. But these types of decisions normally involve several departments or several individuals at various levels of the organization. Thus, relatively more sophisticated models, e.g., portfolio models, could be applied to prioritize the projects, with the NI process being used as a framework for bridging the various parties in a face-to-face decision making setting.

5.10. REFERENCES

1. Souder, W. E. "Effectiveness of Nominal and Interacting Group Decision Processes for Integrating R&D and Marketing," *Management Science*, Vol. 23, No. 6, 1977, pp. 595–605.
2. Souder, W. E. "Achieving Organizational Consensus With Respect to R&D Project Selection Criteria," *Management Science*, Vol. 21, No. 6, 1975, pp. 669–691.
3. Souder, W. E. *Management Decision Methods for Managers of Engineering and Research*. New York: Van Nostrand Reinhold, 1980, pp. 47–78, 135–190, 273–298.
4. Murdick, R. G. and D. W. Karger. "The Shoestring Approach to Rating New Products," *Machine Design*, January 25, 1973, pp. 816–89.
5. Augood, Derek. "A Review of R&D Evaluation Methods," *IEEE Transactions on Engineering Management*, Vol. EM-20, No. 4, 1973, pp. 114–120.
6. Harris, J. S., "Evaluating New Project Proposals," *Chemical and Engineering News*, Vol. 15, No. 8, April 17, 1961.
7. Moore, J. R. and N. R. Baker. "Computational Analysis of Scoring Models for R&D Project Selection," *Management Science*, Vol. 16, No. 6, December, 1969, pp. B212–232.
8. Moore, J. R. and N. R. Baker. "An Analytical Approach to Scoring Model Design —Application to Research and Development Project Selection," *IEEE Transactions on Engineering Management*, Vol. EM-16, No. 3, August, 1969, pp. 90–98.
9. Souder, W. E. "Field Studies With a Q-Sort/Nominal Group Process for Selecting R&D Projects," *Research Policy*, Vol. 5, No. 4, 1975, pp. 172–188.
10. Souder, W. E. "A System for Using R&D Project Evaluation Methods," *Research Management*, Vol. 21, No. 5, 1978, pp. 29–37.
11. Souder, W. E. "Comparative Analysis of R&D Investment Models," *AIIE Transactions*, Vol. 1, No. 2, March, 1972, pp. 57–64.
12. Souder, W. E. "Selecting and Staffing R&D Projects Via Op Research," *Chemical Engineering Progress*, Vol. 63, No. 11, 1967, pp. 27–37.
13. Clarke, T. C. "Decision Making in Technologically Based Organizations; A Literature Survey of Present Practices," *IEEE Transactions on Engineering Management*, Vol. EM-21, No. 1, 1974, pp. 9–23.
14. Gear, A. E., A. G. Lockett, and A. W. Pearson. "Analysis of Some Portfolio Selection Models for R&D," *IEEE Transactions on Engineering Management*, Vol. EM-18, No. 2, 1971, pp. 66–76.
15. Souder, W. E. "Scoring Methodology for Assessing the Suitability of Management Science Models," *Management Science*, Vol. 18, No. 10, June, 1972, pp. B526–543.
16. Dean, B. V. "Evaluating, Selecting and Controlling R&D Projects." American Management Association, New York, Research Study 89, 1968.
17. Souder, W. E. "Selecting and Staffing R&D Projects Via Operations Research," *Chemical Engineering Progress*, Vol. 63, No. 11, November, 1967, pp. 27–37.

6. Basic Economic Appraisal Techniques

6.0. ROLE OF ECONOMIC APPRAISAL TECHNIQUES

Chapter 5 presented several techniques and approaches for screening, evaluating, and selecting new project proposals and ideas. Because of their embryonic state of development, new proposals and ideas often cannot be analyzed in great economic detail. Their market potentials, development costs, likelihoods of success, profitability potentials and other salient attributes may be very difficult to quantify at their early life stage. Thus, the techniques presented in Chapter 5 are more suited to the early-life appraisal of new product ideas and new project proposals.

When market potential, profitability, cost, and other salient data are available on a project or idea, then detailed economic appraisals may be made. Engineering projects, capital equipment and expansion proposals, late-life project developments, investment proposals and modifications to existing products are examples of some types of projects where sufficient data are usually available to apply economic appraisal methods. Note that the approaches presented in Chapter 5 may usefully be applied to these types of projects as well. It is simply that, when the data are available, economic analysis methods should be used because they are more powerful and more rigorous.

This chapter presents the basic methods and techniques of economic appraisal. Chapter 7 demonstrates the application of these methods to project appraisal and selection problems.

6.1. THE ECONOMIC APPRAISAL PERSPECTIVE

Economic appraisal deals with the economic why, the economic when, and the economic how of a project or venture. Economic appraisal deals with the project selection problem (the why): Should this alternative be done at all? Why do we want it? Is it economical? Economic appraisal deals with the timing of the alternatives (the when): Would it be better to do it later? If we do it now, when will we get the economic benefits? And, economic appraisal deals with the apportionment of the investment (the how): Do we want to do all of it now? Is it better to divide up the investment over several periods, or to do it all in one time period?

The focus of economic appraisal is on the *differential* values, the *least complex* independent entity, the *opportunity costs*, and the *incremental costs*. Only those values or costs that are different from one alternative to another (differential) need be considered and carried along throughout the analyses and the decision making. The focus on these differential values simplifies the analyses and centers attention on the most relevant aspects.

The economic appraisal process focuses on the least complex independent entities of the entire system. For example, the decision to buy a new plant may be independent from the purchase of the equipment that will go with it. Decisions such as this (they are separable) are treated independently. This requires each independent element of the decision to "pay its own way."

Economic appraisal focuses on opportunity costs: the lost value of a foregone alternative. For instance, suppose I choose to put my savings in a bank at 6% per annum interest. I may do so because it's safer than my other alternative of buying XYZ Company stock, which yields 10%. I have foregone a differential of 4% in interest, my opportunity cost, for reasons of safety.

The focus is on what is happening as increments of funds are expended, as opposed to the entire amount. This piecemeal approach permits the decision maker to look at the productivity of each incremental dollar expended. Dealing with totals and averages may mask important changes in the increments [1, 2, 3].

6.2. THE ECONOMIC APPRAISAL APPROACH

Most economic appraisals involve five phases of activity: problem definition, information collection, economic analysis, irreducibles analysis, and decision making. The interrelationships between these five phases and the activities they embody are outlined in Figure 6.1.

Note that the phases vary in their degree of management involvement. For instance, the problem definition and decision making phases require top management input, guidance and participation. The other phases are largely within the domain of lower organizational levels, and several levels of the organization will normally become involved.

The phases also vary in the degree of collective wisdom and group inputs required. The problem definition and information collection phases will normally involve several different departments, groups, and individuals. The other phases may require no more than one person. Thus, many of the human behavioral and organizational factors noted in Chapter 5 may also influence the economic appraisal process.

The nature and levels of the analyses also vary with the phases. Problem definition is a strategic-level analysis. Information collection and solicitation often involve detailed data collection, estimation and subjective appraisal methods. Economic analyses activities are usually highly mathematical. In contrast, the irreducibles analysis is heuristic. (Irreducibles, as already discussed, are those aspects that cannot be reduced to monetary terms, and must thus be analyzed subjectively.) Hence, in an economic appraisal, intuition and judgment must be integrated with the numerical analyses.

As shown by the arrows in Figure 6.1, the phases are dynamically interrelated. The conduct of the economic analyses may stimulate a

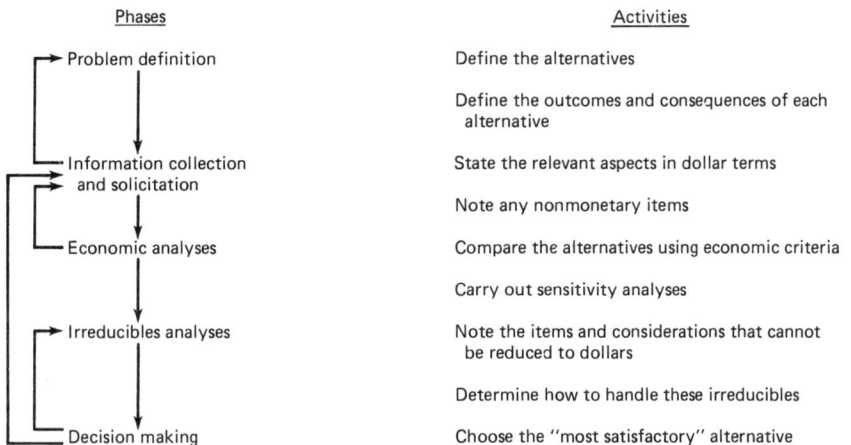

Phases	Activities
Problem definition	Define the alternatives
	Define the outcomes and consequences of each alternative
Information collection and solicitation	State the relevant aspects in dollar terms
	Note any nonmonetary items
Economic analyses	Compare the alternatives using economic criteria
	Carry out sensitivity analyses
Irreducibles analyses	Note the items and considerations that cannot be reduced to dollars
	Determine how to handle these irreducibles
Decision making	Choose the "most satisfactory" alternative

Figure 6.1. Phases and activities in a typical economic appraisal.

search for additional information. The information collection process may suggest a restatement and reformulation of the problem, etc.

In practice, the activities within the phases may be difficult to carry out. The problem definition phase assumes that several alternatives are known, and that their outcomes and consequences can be listed. Some economic problems are so uncertain and unstructured that these conditions are not met. Similarly, information collection and solicitation may be a major obstacle unless the problem is well-defined. It may be difficult to phrase the relevant aspects in the desired objective of measurable monetary units. In fact, many of the key aspects of economic problems are often irreducibles.

Thus, while economic appraisal methods are valuable and highly useful for quantifying some aspects of project selection and appraisal problems, judgment and intuition must still be applied. The proper role of economic appraisal methods is to assist in the decision process, by limiting the use of intuition and subjective assessments to only those factors requiring such treatment [1, 2, 3].

6.3. ECONOMIC APPRAISAL CONCEPTS

Because money has a time value, a dollar today is not equivalent to a dollar one year from today. To illustrate, suppose we are given a choice between two investment projects, A and B. Let us further assume these two projects are alike in every respect, except that project A returns its profits one year earlier. Clearly, project A is the preferred project. The earlier returns from project A can be reinvested to produce additional time-related profits.

Project appraisals frequently involve the manipulation and comparison of monetary data and dollar amounts taken from different time periods. Like the old saying about comparing apples and oranges, dollar amounts taken from different time periods are not directly comparable. Rather, they must first be *equivalenced*, or placed on a comparable time-value scale.

6.3.1. The Equivalence Concept

At an annual interest rate of $i\%$, the present worth of $1.00 today is equivalent to a future worth of $1.00 + $1.00 \times i\%$ one year from today. This is the equivalence concept. Note that it has nothing to do with risk and inflation. Even in an inflationless and riskless situation, money will still have a time value.

In general, the future worth F of a lump sum of money at the end of n years is equivalenced to a present worth P by the relationship

$$P = F\left(\frac{1}{(1 + i)^n}\right), \qquad (6.1)$$

where i is an annual interest rate. Inversely, P is equivalenced to F by the relationship

$$F = P(1 + i)^n. \qquad (6.2)$$

The factor $(1 + i)^n$ is the *compound amount factor*, and its inverse $1/(1 + i)^n$ is the *discount factor*. To illustrate, \$2,000 invested for 10 years at 6% annual interest will appreciate to (or is equivalent to) a future worth of

$$F = \$2,000(1.06)^{10} = \$3,581.70.$$

Alternatively, \$3,581.70 received ten years from today is equivalent to

$$P = \$3,581.70/(1.06)^{10} = \$2,000$$

received today. That is, \$2,000 is the present worth equivalent of \$3,581.70.

In the case where there is a stream of annual amounts $A_1, A_2, \ldots, A_n$ invested at the start of years $1, 2, \ldots, n$ and where $A_1 = A_2 = \ldots A_n = A$, then

$$A = F\left(\frac{i}{(1 + i)^n - 1}\right), \qquad (6.3)$$

and

$$F = A\left(\frac{(1 + i)^n - 1}{i}\right). \qquad (6.4)$$

This can be seen by noting that $F = A_1(1 + i)^n + A_2(1 + i)^{n-1} + \cdots + A_n(1 + i)$, and using algebraic reduction [2, 4]. By substituting equation (6.2) into equation (6.4) and using algebraic reduction we obtain

$$A = P\left(\frac{i(1 + i)^n}{(1 + i)^n - 1}\right), \tag{6.5}$$

and

$$P = A\left(\frac{(1 + i)^n - 1}{i(1 + i)^n}\right). \tag{6.6}$$

Note that the factor $i(1 + i)^n/[(1 + i)^n - 1]$ is called the *capital recovery factor* because it gives the stream of withdrawals of capital plus interest supplied over time period n by an equivalent P.

6.3.2. Examples and Illustrations

To illustrate these basic concepts, suppose I wish to calculate how much money I will have 10 years from now if I deposit $10,000 in a bank account at an annual interest rate of 12%. From equation (6.2),

$$F = \$10,000(1.12)^{10} = \$31,058.48.$$

By comparison, if I had set up a program of depositing $1,000 per year at the start of each year, using equation (6.4), I would have accumulated only

$$F = \$1,000\left(\frac{(1.12)^{10} - 1}{0.12}\right) = \$17,548.74.$$

To further illustrate these concepts, suppose I have decided to retire, and I am faced with deciding between two retirement income alternatives. I can have either a lump sum payment of $10,000 or an annuity that pays $1,000 per year for the next 10 years. Let $i = 12\%$. From equation (6.6),

$$P = \$1,000 \left(\frac{(1.12)^{10} - 1}{(0.12)(1.12)^{10}} \right) = \$5,650.22.$$

This indicates that the annuity is far inferior to the $10,000 lump sum. Note that the $10,000 and $5,650.22 amounts are on a comparable scale, and can be directly compared. Note that another acceptable (but more tedious) way to make this comparison would be to compute

$$F = \$10,000(1.12)^{10} = \$31,058.48$$

and compare it with

$$F = \$1,000 \left(\frac{(1.12)^{10} - 1}{0.12} \right) = \$17,548.74.$$

This leads to the same decision: the lump sum alternative is superior to the annuity.

6.3.3. Handling The Factors

Equivalencing factors are best viewed as ways to convert given variables into desired variables. For example, given a present value, suppose a series value A is desired. We may set up this problem as follows:

$$\frac{\text{Desired}}{\text{Variable}} = \frac{\text{Given}}{\text{Variable}} \times \text{factor}$$

$$A = P \times \text{?}$$

Using label cancellation techniques, it is obvious that we want the A/P factor since:

$$A = P \times A/P$$

Recall from equation (6.5) that $A/P = i(1 + i)^n / [(1 + i)^n - 1]$. Thus, by label cancellation methods, we can always be assured of selecting the correct factor.

To illustrate, suppose I wish to ascertain a ten-year retirement annuity plan based on an initial investment of $100,000 at 6% annual interest. Hence, P is the given variable, and A is the desired variable. Thus,

$$A = \$100,000 \left(\frac{0.06(1.06)^{10}}{(1.06)^{10} - 1} \right) = \$13,596.80.$$

Hence, $13,596.80 is the amount I can expect to withdraw at the end of each year for 10 years from an escrow account of $100,000, and have a zero balance at the end of the 10th year.

Table 6.1 lists the various factors and their ratio labels. This table is a useful guide for setting up the label cancellation equations.

Equivalence calculations may be readily carried out on an electronic pocket calculator, a programmable calculator, or a small computer. Tabled values of the F/P, P/F, etc. factors are also available for most interest rates, so that the user need only look up the value of the factor that is needed [2, 3, 4]. The tables economize on the amount of calculations required.

6.3.4. Compounding Periods

It is not unusual for interest rates to be expressed on an annual basis, while being compounded semiannually, quarterly or on some other periodic basis. In general,

$$i = r/m, \tag{6.7}$$

where r is the *nominal interest rate* in percentage terms, expressed on an annual basis and i is the *effective interest rate* in percentage terms,

Table 6.1. Equivalencing Factors.

DESIRED VARIABLE	GIVEN VARIABLE	ALGEBRAIC FACTOR	RATIO LABEL	EQUATION
P	F	$1/(1 + i)^n$	P/F	(6.1)
F	P	$(1 + i)^n$	F/P	(6.2)
A	F	$i/[(1 + i)^n - 1]$	A/F	(6.3)
F	A	$[(1 + i)^n - 1]/i$	F/A	(6.4)
A	P	$[i(1 + i)^n]/[(1 + i)^n - 1]$	A/P	(6.5)
P	A	$[(1 + i)^n - 1]/[i(1 + i)^n]$	P/A	(6.6)

corresponding to the actual compounding period. The factor m is the number of interest periods per year. In all the previous calculations above, it was assumed that $m = 1$, so that $i = r$. In general when $m > 1$, equations (6.1) through (6.6) respectively become:

$$P = F\left(\frac{1}{[1 + (r/m)]^{mn}}\right) \tag{6.8}$$

$$F = P[1 + (r/m)]^{mn} \tag{6.9}$$

$$A = mF\left(\frac{r/m}{[1 + (r/m)]^{mn} - 1}\right) \tag{6.10}$$

$$F = \frac{A}{m}\left(\frac{[1 + (r/m)]^{mn} - 1}{r/m}\right) \tag{6.11}$$

$$A = mP\left(\frac{(r/m)[1 + (r/m)]^{mn}}{(1 + r/m)^{mn} - 1}\right) \tag{6.12}$$

$$P = \frac{A}{m}\left(\frac{[1 + (r/m)]^{mn} - 1}{(r/m)[1 + (r/m)]^{mn}}\right). \tag{6.13}$$

As an example, let us return to the illustration in Section 6.3.2 above, with the $5,650.22 present value annuity. Suppose the interest had been compounded quarterly and the annuity paid quarterly instead of annually. Then from equation (6.13),

$$P = \$250\left[\frac{(1.03)^{40} - 1}{(0.03)(1.03)^{40}}\right] = \$5,778.69.$$

Hence, quarterly compounding makes a small difference in this example, as it typically does.

In some cases, continuous compounding is used [2, 4]. Then,

$$i = e^r - 1, \tag{6.14}$$

where e is the base of the natural system of logarithms, equal to 2.7182. Hence, when continuous compounding is used, equation (6.2) becomes $F = P(e^{rn})$. Equation (6.4) becomes

$$F = A\left[\frac{e^{rn} - 1}{e^r - 1}\right].$$

Equation (6.5) becomes

$$A = P\left[\frac{e^r - 1}{1 - e^{-rn}}\right].$$

And so on.

6.3.5. The Choice of an Interest Rate

There is no one interest rate that is most appropriate for use in equivalence calculations. If the decision maker is lending money, then $i\%$ should be the prevailing or market rate for lending one's own money. If the decision maker is borrowing money, then $i\%$ should be the prevailing or market rate for borrowing someone else's money. Note that these rates are seldom the same, e.g., a bank will charge a borrower a higher rate than they will pay a depositor.

If a firm is financing a new investment from internally generated funds, then $i\%$ may be set to the firm's average return on current investments. The logic behind this choice is simple: the new investment should be at least as good as the current ones. If this is not the case, then the decision maker has incurred an opportunity cost. The opportunity cost is the amount by which the new investment is inferior. For example, suppose I can obtain 12% annual interest from depositing my money in a bank and 10% annual return by investing in antiques. By investing in antiques, I have foregone an opportunity to earn 12%. I have thus incurred an opportunity cost of $12\% - 10\% = 2\%$. The 12% rate must be considered the standard for judging other alternative opportunities. It is the *opportunity cost rate*. Note that it is not always illogical to purposely incur opportunity costs in the short run, e.g., starting up a new business. But the decision maker who unwittingly takes such paper losses may soon find himself in very poor shape. Note also that I may decide that the 2% rate differential is not a significant cost vis-à-vis the amenities, or the so-called irreducible benefits that I obtain from the pleasures of collecting antiques.

The interest rate $i\%$ may also be set at some target level above the return on current investments. This would be the case where management wishes to discount future earnings more heavily than current and past earnings. For example, suppose a new investment is expected to produce a stream of future earnings $A_1, A_2, \ldots, A_n$ and $j\%$ is the current return on investment rate. If this new investment is more risky than the current ones, management may feel that a risk premium of $k\%$ should be added to bring the target rate up to $i\% = j\% + k\%$. In essence, this target rate (or hurdle rate, as it is often called) is the level that management feels they should have to compensate them for the added risk of the new investment.

6.3.6. Rate Adjustments for Taxes and Inflation

When interest is being compounded in an inflationary economy, a composite interest rate $v\%$ may be used in equivalence calculations [2, 3, 4]. In general,

$$v = (i - p)/(1 + p) \tag{6.15}$$

where p is the annual inflation rate. All the above equations may be used with $v\%$ in place of $i\%$.

If interest is taxed at a rate t and interest costs are tax deductible, then the net interest rate returned to an investor, and the net interest rate paid by a borrower, is given by

$$(1 - t)i. \tag{6.16}$$

This factor may also be incorporated into the equivalence calculations. For example, the after-tax, after-inflation composite interest rate factor g is given by

$$g = [(1 - t)i - p]/(1 + p). \tag{6.17}$$

6.4. ECONOMIC APPRAISAL MODELS

6.4.1. The Equivalent Uniform Annual Cost (EUAC) Model

This model is especially useful for comparing costs in different time periods. The model is:

$$A = P(A/P) - S(A/F) \tag{6.18}$$

where A is the equivalent uniform annual cost (EUAC), P is the gross first cost, and S is the net salvage value. Other algebraically equivalent formulae for the EUAC model are:

$$A = P(A/P) - S[(A/P) - i] \tag{6.19}$$

$$A = (P - S)(A/P) + Si \tag{6.20}$$

$$A = (P - S)(A/F) + Pi. \tag{6.21}$$

Here, i is the opportunity cost rate. Equation (6.18) is perhaps the most logical version of the EUAC model, while equation (6.21) is the most computationally efficient.

To illustrate the EUAC model, let us consider that the data in Table 6.2 represent three alternative financing plans for producing widgets. Plan A is labor intensive, plan B is capital intensive, and plan C represents a fully automated production line. The company management believes it can get an 8% per annum return on project D, which is competing for the widget project funds. The company management has decided to go into widget production as part of a long range market penetration strategy. Therefore, the problem is: "Which is the least cost plan for widgets?"

Figure 6.2 is a plot of the cash flows required for each plan. Clearly, as shown in Figure 6.2, the three plans do not have the same cash

Table 6.2. EUAC Model Data.

	PLAN A	PLAN B	PLAN C
Data:			
First cost of equipment	—	$150,000*	$250,000*
Annual labor cost	$92,000	$ 33,000	$ 17,000
Annual operating & maintenance	—	$ 31,000	$ 40,500
Equipment salvage value	—	0	$ 50,000**
Opportunity cost rate (project D)	8%	8%	8%
Analysis:			
$A =$	$92,000	$ 86,350	$ 91,310
Decision: B > C > A, based on the equivalent uniform annual cost (EUAC).			

* 10-year life.
** At end of 10-year life.

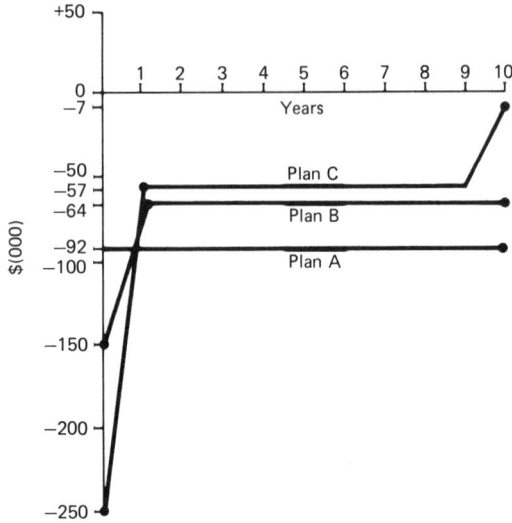

Figure 6.2. Cash flow profiles of plans A, B, and C from Table 6.2.

flow over the 10 year planning horizon. Plan B creates a relatively small ($64,000) constant cash drain, but requires a large ($150,000) initial outlay. Plan C has the smallest ($57,000) constant cash drain, with a $50,000 cash inflow in ycar 10, thus giving it a net flow of −$7,500 in year 10. But plan C requires a very large ($250,000) initial outlay. Thus, it is clear that the three plans can only be compared on some equivalent basis. An appropriate equivalent basis for a "least cost choice" decision of this type is the EUAC model.

Plan A is already stated on an annualized cost basis. Thus, only plans B and C need be put on an equivalent annualized cost basis. For Plan B:

$$A = \$150,000(A/P) + \$64,000$$

$$= \$150,000 \left(\frac{i(1 + i)^n}{(1 + i)^n - 1} \right) + \$64,000$$

$$= \$150,000 \left(\frac{(0.08)(1.08)^{10}}{(1.08)^{10} - 1} \right) + \$64,000$$

$$= \$86,350.$$

For plan C:

$$A = \$250,000(A/P) + \$57,500 - \$50,000(A/F)$$

$$= \$91,310.$$

Note how the salvage value is handled: $\$50,000 \times A/F = \$3,410$. Thus, the release of \$50,000 in the 10th year is equivalent to having \$3,410 in *each* of the 10 years. The difference, \$5,000 per year minus \$3,410 per year, is the annual equivalent opportunity cost of capital tied up for 10 years at the 8% rate.

As shown at the bottom of Table 6.2, plan B is the best choice, based on the criterion of lowest EUAC (the symbol > is read "is preferred to"). The implicit opportunity costs on the invested capital make the automated plan C relatively unattractive. The high cost of labor makes the labor-intensive plan A unattractive relative to both B and C.

This example illustrates the general idea that there usually exists an optimum labor to capital ratio for total cost minimization. This optimum should be sought out by analyzing several cases. It is also essential to check the sensitivity of the decision to changes in the critical parameters. For example, the preference ordering of plans A, B, and C will change if $i = 15\%$. In that case, the imputed opportunity costs of the invested capital for plans B and C are so great relative to plan A that A > B > C. In some cases, the best-choice plan will be dominant throughout the range of variations in the critical parameters. Where reversals in choices occur under varations in the critical parameters, as in the preceding example, the decision maker may have to resolve the quandry intuitively. That is, the final decision as to the best plan may involve an intuitive assessment of the risk that the variations will in fact actually occur, and a willingness to accept such risks.

Finally, it must be noted that analyses like the above necessarily contain certain limitations. For example, in the analysis just given, no allowance was made for year to year fluctuations in operating costs and maintenance schedules. Also, it is not very likely that interest rates, and hence, the opportunity cost of capital rate, will remain constant over the 10 year horizon. However, unless the alternatives are very nearly equal-valued, these limitations will not significantly affect the results.

Irreducibles, which cannot be monetized and explicitly put into the equations, may have a more significant impact on the final decision. In the above example, some relevant irreducibles in favor of plan C might include a desire to gain experience with automated systems, a desire to reduce the influence of labor and/or a union, and the expectation that plan C could lead to more advanced automated systems that have relatively lower capital costs. Economic appraisal computations cannot directly help the decision maker analyze such irreducibles. However, economic appraisal techniques can determine whether or not the irreducibles that separate two alternatives are adequate to counterbalance the opportunity cost incurred in choosing the more costly alternative. For example, the analysis of the data in Table 6.2 shows that the decision maker who takes plan C over B incurs an annual opportunity cost of $91,310 - $86,350 = $4,960. With this knowledge, the decision maker may be better able to intuit whether it really is worthwhile to accept plan C over plan B.

6.4.2. The Present Worth (PW) Model

The PW model is:

$$P = A(P/A) + S(P/F), \qquad (6.22)$$

where S is the salvage value, P is the present worth, and A is the annual cash flow. To illustrate, suppose we have two choices, plan 1 and plan 2. Both plans cost the same. Plan 1 will generate an annual cash flow of $6,000 per year for 10 years. Plan 2 will generate an annual cash flow of $5,000 per year for 12 years. Plan 2 will also return a lump sum of $11,000 in the 12th year. Let us assume an interest rate of 10%. Then the present worths P_1 and P_2 of the two plans are, respectively:

$$P_1 = \$6,000(P/A)$$

$$= \$6,000\left(\frac{(1.10)^{10} - 1}{(0.10)(1.10)^{10}}\right) = \$36,867.40$$

$$P_2 = \$5,000(P/A) + \$11,000(P/F)$$

$$= \$5,000\left(\frac{(1.10)^{12} - 1}{(0.10)(1.10)^{12}}\right) + \$11,000\left(\frac{1}{(1.10)^{12}}\right)$$

$$= \$37,573.40$$

Hence, Plan 2 is superior to Plan 1: it has a higher present worth. Note that, because of the small margin of difference between Plans 1 and 2, the sensitivity of this decision to changes in interest rates and other parameters should be checked.

Let us now return to the illustration in Table 6.2 and Figure 6.2. Although the absolute magnitudes of the numbers are different, the same decision results for plans A, B, and C if they are analyzed in terms of the PW cost equivalency and the EUAC equivalency models. Specifically, for plan A,

$$P = \$92,000(P/A) = \$617,300;$$

For plan B,

$$P = \$150,000 + \$64,000(P/A) = \$579,400;$$

For plan C,

$$P = \$250,000 + \$57,500(P/A) - \$50,000(P/F)$$

$$- \$612,699.$$

Note that, since we are dealing with costs, for plan C the $50,000 cash inflow is subtracted.

Thus, the present worth cost model leads to $B > C > A$. The preference ordering of the alternative choices will always be the same under both the EUAC and PW models. This is because the two models differ by a constant factor. Then why do we need both models? The answer is that sometimes one of the two is easier to use. As a general rule, the PW model is easiest to use in those cases where the performance data (e.g., operating and maintenance costs) are variable over the planning horizon. The EUAC model is more computationally efficient for comparing alternatives with unequal lives. The EUAC model is also the simplest to use for assets with lives of 50 years or more, because the A/P factor approaches the interest rate for $n > 50$. In that case, $A/P \approx i$, and the calculations are greatly simplified.

6.4.3. Return On Investment Models

In both the PW and EUAC models we were concerned with *either* costs (outlays, disbursements, etc.) *or* returns (values that flow into the business). In return on investment models, we are concerned with handling *both* costs and returns.

There are four commonly used return on investment models. They are: the internal rate of return, the net present value, the payback period, and the financial percent return on investment. Let us now examine each of these models.

6.4.4. The Internal Rate of Return (IRR) Model

Let us take the PW model from equation (6.22) and algebraically transform it into

$$0 = -P + A(P/A) + S(P/F),$$

$$= -P + A\left(\frac{(1 + i)^n - 1}{(i)(1 + i)^n}\right) + S\left(\frac{1}{(1 + i)^n}\right). \qquad (6.23)$$

Equation (6.23) is the *internal rate of return* (IRR) model. For a given value of n, the value of i which solves the equation, call it i^*, is referred to as the internal rate of return (IRR). Or, restating equation (6.23), the IRR is the value of i which equivalences the outlays P with the receipts A and S (when S exists).

To illustrate, let us compute the internal rate of return for an investment of \$50,000 that returns \$15,000 per year for five years.

From equation (6.23):

$$0 = -\$50{,}000 + \$15{,}000 \left(\frac{(1+i)^5 - 1}{(i)(1+i)^5} \right)$$

$$= -\$50{,}000 + \$15{,}000(P/A)$$

$$P/A = 3.3333.$$

By calculations (or table look-up) we find the following data:

i	P/A
12%	3.6047
15%	3.3521
20%	2.9906

By linear interpolation from the above data we find:

$$i^* = 15\% + \left(\frac{3.3333 - 3.3521}{3.3521 - 2.9906} \right) \times (20\% - 15\%)$$

$$= 15.26\%.$$

6.4.5. The Net Present Value (NPV) Model

If we choose a value of $i > i^*$, the value of equation (6.23) will be less than 0. If we choose a value of $i < i^*$, the value of equation (6.23) will be greater than 0. For example, given a value of n, for a given value $i \leq i^*$, then

$$X = A \left(\frac{(1+i)^n - 1}{(i)(1+i)^n} \right) + S \left(\frac{1}{(1+i)^n} \right) - P, \tag{6.24}$$

where $X \geq 0$. The value of X in equation (6.24) is the net present value (NPV) of the investment P. Equation (6.24) is the *net present value* (NPV) model. The value X is commonly referred to as the *discounted cash flow* (DCF). Thus, equation (6.24) is often referred to as the DCF model.

To illustrate, let us determine the NPV for the above $50,000 investment at interest rates of 10% (case 1) and 20% (case 2). From equation (6.24):

Case 1: $X = \text{NPV} = -\$50,000 + \$15,000 \left(\dfrac{(1.10)^5 - 1}{(0.10)(1.10)^5} \right)$

$= \$6,861.80$

Case 2: $X = \text{NPV} = -\$50,000 + \$15,000 \left(\dfrac{(1.20)^5 - 1}{(0.20)(1.20)^5} \right)$

$= -\$4,999.70$

6.4.6. The Payback Period (PBP) Model

The *payback period* (PBP) is the time required to recoup the original investment or original cost through the flow of net returns, neglecting the time value of money. In general, the PBP is that j where

$$P = \sum_{j=1}^{\text{PBP}} \text{CF}_j, \tag{6.25}$$

where CF_j is the net cash flow in year j, $j = 1, 2, \ldots, n$. The net cash flow in the jth year consists of the algebraic difference between the costs and the returns in that year.

For example, for the above $50,000 investment, $P = \$50,000$ and $\text{CF}_j = \$15,000$. Thus, PBP $= \$50,000/\$15,000 = 3.33$ years.

6.4.7. The Financial Percent Return on Investment (%ROI)

The *financial percent return on investment* (%ROI) is a given by

$$\%\text{ROI} = \left[\left(\sum_{j=1}^{n} \text{CF}_j - P \right) \Big/ P \right] \times 100\%. \tag{6.26}$$

Thus, the %ROI is the net percent return on investment, ignoring the time value of money. For example, for the above $50,000 investment:

$$\%\text{ROI} = \left(\frac{(5 \times \$15,000) - \$50,000}{\$50,000}\right) \times 100\% = 50\%.$$

Note the significant difference between this result and the above result of 15.26% for the IRR, where the time value of money was taken into account.

6.5. COMPARISON OF RETURN ON INVESTMENT MODELS

Tables 6.3, 6.4, and 6.5 present some comparative results with the above four return on investment models. As shown in Table 6.3, there are four investment proposals: A, B, C, and D. Each proposal requires the same level of investment: $100,000. Proposals A, B, and C each have the same total net cash flow: $100,000. However, the time shape of the flows of the returns at the ends of years 1 through 5 differ. Thus, as shown in Table 6.4, the net present values differ.

6.5.1. Choosing The Best Model

Table 6.5 presents the results from applying the above discussed return on investment models to the data in Tables 6.3 and 6.4. The salient question now is: which of the four models is "best"?

The %ROI model is clearly not sufficient. It does not distinguish between the different time shapes of the cash flows for the proposals.

The payback period model is only partially satisfactory. The payback period model is somewhat sensitive to the time lag between the investment and the returns, e.g., see proposal A versus proposal C. But, it is not sensitive to the time shape, e.g., proposal A versus proposal B. Morever, the payback period model is not influenced by the shape or magnitude of any returns that occur beyond the recovery of the initial investment (returns greater than $100,000, in this case). For example, note that proposal D provides no return on the investment. Only an amount equal to the original investment, $100,000, is returned. Clearly, proposal D is a worse choice than any of the others. Yet this is not adequately reflected in the payback period result.

Table 6.3. Investment Proposals.

END OF	DOLLAR CASH FLOWS $(000) OF THE PROPOSALS			
YEAR	A	B	C	D
0	−100	−100	−100	−100
1	+25	0	0	0
2	+75	+100	0	+100
3	+100	+75	+25	0
4	0	+25	+75	0
5	0	0	+100	0
Net cash flow:	$ 100	$ 100	$ 100	0

Table 6.4. Present Values* of the Data in Table 6.3.

END OF	PRESENT VALUES $(000) OF THE PROPOSALS, AT $i = 10\%$			
YEAR	A	B	C	D
0	−100	−100	−100	−100
1	+22.72	0	0	0
2	+61.98	+82.65	0	+82.65
3	+75.13	+56.34	+18.78	0
4	0	+17.07	+51.22	0
5	0	0	+62.09	0
Net present values:	+59.83	+56.06	+32.09	−17.35

*Let PV_n be the present value for year n. Then: $PV_n = $ (Dollar Cash Flow)$/(1.10)^n$, e.g., for proposal A, $PV_1 = \$25/(1.10) = \$22.72$, $PV_2 = \$75/(1.10)^2 = \$61.98$, etc.

Table 6.5. Results With Four Common Models.

	PROPOSALS			
MODELS	A	B	C	D
Payback	2 yrs.	2 yrs.	4 yrs.	2 yrs.
%ROI	100%	100%	100%	0%
NPV @ $i = 10\%$	$59.83	$56.06	$32.09	$−17.35
IRR*	37%	32%	17%	negative

Conclusion: A > B > C; D is unacceptable; C will not be acceptable if the minimum acceptable rate of return (cut-off point) is above 17%

*these numbers are rounded off

Both the NPV and the IRR models escape all the above deficiencies. Both are perfectly valid models. In fact, they are algebraically equivalent models. The difference is that the NPV model uses a given value for i, whereas the IRR model solves for i^*, a particular value of the variable i. For the data in Table 6.3, if the NPV model is evaluated using the IRR value for i^*, the NPV will be zero. For example, if the NPV computation were repeated for proposal A using $i = 37\%$, the NPV would be zero.[1]

Either the NPV or the IRR model will necessarily lead to the same decision. For example, both the NPV and the IRR models yielded the same conclusion at the foot of Table 6.5: A is a better proposal than B, which is better than C, and D is unacceptable.

6.5.2. Using a Minimum Acceptable Rate of Return (MARR)

Why, then, do we have both the NPV and IRR models? Because in some situations management may have specified a minimum acceptable rate of return (MARR). This could be either the firm's opportunity cost of capital or an artificial rate which effectively serves as a cut-off rate. Where a MARR exists, the NPV can be calculated using $i = $ MARR. If the value of the NPV is negative, the project is unacceptable. Of course, the IRR can also be computed and compared to the MARR. Then if the IRR < MARR the project is unacceptable. But, the NPV value is easier to compute and it always results in a single value.

6.5.3. Other Considerations in Choosing the Best Model

The choice of the "best" return on investment model depends on several factors. These include the accuracy of the data, the reinvestment assumptions, whether or not a MARR has been set, the fuzziness of the MARR criterion, and management's felt need for quick returns [2, 3].

The NPV and IRR models are theoretically correct models for every circumstance, in that they explicitly take the time value of

---

[1] Theoretically this should always be true [1, 2, 4]. However, solutions to IRR model equations may have more than one root since the factor $(1 + i)^n$ will lead to quadratic, quartic, etc. equations for $n > 1$. In general, cash flow streams which have reversals in signs often lead to multiple values for i^*.

Table 6.6. Corresponding Models for Various Types of Decisions.

TYPE OF DECISION	APPROPRIATE MODEL
Least cost alternative	Model: EUAC Formula: $$A = P(A/P) - S(A/F)$$ where A is the annual equivalent cost, P is an outlay cost and S is the salvage value. Criterion: Choose the alternative with the lowest A value.
Greatest value alternative	Model: PW Formula: $$P = -A(P/A) + S(P/F)$$ where P is the equivalent present value, A is the annual cost, and S is the salvage value. Criterion: Choose the alternative with the highest P value.
Return on investment, MARR given	Model: NPV Formula: $$NPV = -P + A(P/A) + S(P/F) @ i$$ where i is the MARR value, A is the annual cost, S is the salvage value, and P is the investment. Criterion: Choose the alternative with largest positive NPV.
Return on investment, MARR not given	Model: IRR Formula: $$0 = -P + A(P/A) + S(P/F)$$ Solve for i^*, the value of i that satisfies the equation, where the variables are the same as in the NPV model. Criterion: Choose the alternative with the largest i^* value.

money into account. However, the payback period model, in spite of its serious inadequacies, often must be given some consideration. Let's take an extreme illustration of a cash-poor firm. A project with exponentially increasing returns that start in year 8 may be rejected in favor of a more modest project whose returns begin immediately. Even though the IRR of the former project may be superior, the firm may be compelled to select the modest project because it cannot afford to wait for the payback. Hence, in most cases, either the IRR or the NPV is the primary model, with secondary consideration given to the payback period model [2, 3].

6.6. SUMMARY AND CONCLUSIONS

Table 6.6 summarizes the appropriate models to use for the minimum cost, maximum value, and maximum return on investment types of decisions. The formulas are for single increments of outlays, investments, etc., and can be modified appropriately to include multiple increments. For example, the EUAC formula in Table 6.6 can be extended to include multiple outlays in years 1, 2, $\ldots$, m for m $<$ n, and salvage values in years 8, 9, $\ldots$, n, as follows:

$$A = P_1 \left(\frac{(i)(1+i)}{(1+i)-1} \right) + P_2 \left(\frac{(i)(1+i)^2}{(1+i)^2-1} \right) + \cdots$$

$$+ P_m \left(\frac{(i)(1+i)^m}{(1+i)^m-1} \right) - S_8 \left(\frac{i}{(1+i)^8-1} \right)$$

$$- S_9 \left(\frac{i}{(1+i)^9-1} \right) - \cdots - S_n \left(\frac{i}{(1+i)^n-1} \right).$$

It may be noted that the EUAC formula may be used to compute an annual equivalent *value* A and the PW formula may be used to compute a present worth *cost* P. In that case, the appropriate definitions and corresponding algebraic signs must be used for each variable, e.g., if a present worth cost is being computed, the PW formula becomes

$$P = A(P/A) - S(P/F)$$

where A and P are costs and S is a value. It may be noted that the four formulas in Table 6.6 are all algebraically equivalent.

6.7. REFERENCES

1. Souder, W. E. *Management Decision Methods for Managers of Engineering and Research.* New York: Van Nostrand Reinhold, 1980, pp. 100–134.
2. Gottfried, B. G. and W. E. Souder. *Engineering Economy.* New York: McGraw-Hill, 1983.
3. Souder, W. E. "Project Selection", Chapter 10 of *Project Management Handbook*, D. Cleland, ed., Van Nostrand Reinhold: New York, 1983.
4. Fabrycky, W. J. and G. J. Thuesen. *Economic Decision Analysis.* New Jersey: Prentice-Hall, 1979.

7. Economic Appraisal and Selection of Projects

7.0. APPLICATIONS OF ECONOMIC APPRAISAL TECHNIQUES

Chapter 6 presented the basic concepts and methods of economic appraisal. This chapter illustrates the application of these techniques to several common types of project selection problems.

7.1. MUTUALLY EXCLUSIVE PROJECTS

One of the most significant decisions that every firm makes is the choice among mutually exclusive projects or proposals. A typical example of this type of decision is the decision to undertake new plant expansions or new capital investments [1].

Table 7.1. Algorithm for Analyzing Mutually Exclusive Projects and Proposals.

STEP NUMBER	ACTIVITY
1	Array the candidates from smallest to largest size dollar investment.
2	Eliminate from further consideration any candidate whose $i^* <$ MARR.
3	From the remaining candidates, select as the standard the candidate with the smallest size dollar investment.
4	Compute the Δi^* between the standard and the next larger (in terms of size of investment) challenger.
5	If $\Delta i^* \leq$ MARR, eliminate this challenger and repeat step 4; if $\Delta i^* >$ MARR, replace the old standard with this challenger and repeat step 4.
6	Select the best alternative(s) such that: (a) $\Delta i^* \geq$ MARR (b) the total investment $\leq$ total budget.

Intuitively, one would expect that the optimum decision rule is to simply select the proposal with the largest total return on its investment. But this is *incorrect*. The project exhibiting the largest *total* return on investment is *not necessarily* the best choice. A correct procedure is outlined in Table 7.1.

7.1.1. Example: Capital Equipment Selection[1]

The data in Table 7.2 are for five different alternative sizes of a processor machine. The company confronted with a choice among these 5 machines is attempting to ascertain the "best" size investment (machine), given a total capital budget of $250,000 and a minimum acceptable rate of return (MARR) of 15%.

Following step 1 of the algorithm outlined in Table 7.1, the five alternatives are arrayed from left to right in Table 7.2 in terms of smallest to largest present value total investment. Continuing in Table 7.2, applying step 2 of the algorithm eliminates the economy size because its IRR < MARR. This is clearly reasonable: it makes no sense to retain any alternative whose i^* is below the minimum acceptable rate.

Continuing in Table 7.2, step 3 of the algorithm then requires that the regular size machine be selected as the standard, since it represents the smallest amount of funds we can spend. Then, in step 4, the standard is checked against the next larger sized challenger.

7.1.2. Incremental Calculations and the MARR

Why, specifically, must we use the next larger sized investment (machine) as the challenger? The answer is: because we want to check *each successive incremental* expenditure, in that order. Unless the next *incremental* expenditure is as productive as the opportunity represented by the MARR, then we won't make the expenditure. This is the rationale behind step 4.

Note that the value Δi^* computed in step 4 is the incremental return on investment or incremental productivity of capital. For example, in the super versus regular comparison,

$$\Delta i^* = (\$36,000 - \$25,000)/(\$200,000 - \$100,000) = 0.11 < MARR.$$

---

[1] This example is based on the author's case studies which appear in References 1 and 2, reprinted by permission.

Table 7.2. Example With Mutually Exclusive Proposals.

FIVE SIZES OF A PROCESSOR MACHINE, EACH HAVING A LIFETIME
OF 60 YEARS AND NO SALVAGE VALUE

	ECONOMY	REGULAR	SUPER	DELUXE	SUPER-DELUXE
Present value of total lifetime returns, $R =$	$ 5,000	$ 25,000	$ 36,000	$ 45,000	$ 48,000
Present value of total investment, $I =$	$50,000	$100,000	$200,000	$220,000	$250,000
IRR[a], $i^* =$	0%	25%	18%	20.45%	19.2%
Step 2:	Unacceptable	Acceptable	Acceptable	Acceptable	Acceptable
Step 3:		Standard #1	Challenger #1		

Budget = $250,000
MARR = 15%

Step 4:
$$\Delta i^* = \frac{\$11,000}{\$100,000} = 0.11 < \text{MARR}^{b}$$

Step 5: Standard #1 .... Challenger #2
$$\Delta i^* = \frac{\$20,000}{\$120,000} = 0.167 > \text{MARR}^{c}$$

Step 5 repeat: Standard #2 .... Challenger #3
$$\Delta i^* = \frac{\$3,000}{\$30,000} = 0.10 < \text{MARR}^{d}$$

Step 6: Conclusion—Buy the deluxe machine.

[a] Note that for $n = 60$, $A/P \approx i^*$; thus, IRR $\approx R/I$ for all machine sizes.
[b] By Step 5, challenger #1 is eliminated because $\Delta i^* < $ MARR.
[c] By Step 5, standard #1 is replaced by standard #2 because $\Delta i^* > $ MARR.
[d] By Step 5, standard #2 wins.

Hence, the regular size machine is economically superior to the super size machine because the incremental return on the super is less than the MARR. What sense does this make? Let us look at the rationale. Suppose we buy the regular machine and "save" the $100,000 difference. Management has stipulated that this $100,000 can be invested at (or is otherwise worth) 15%—the MARR. Where the MARR represents an actual alternative opportunity available to the company, then there is an actual opportunity loss of $15\% - 11\% = 4\%$ on the $100,000 (or $4,000) in selecting the super size machine. Where there is no such actual opportunity, the loss is no less real to the management that has set the MARR at 15% in order to save for contingencies, or to lock out low return alternatives, etc. Thus, whatever the rationale for the specified value of the MARR, its use as a cutoff criterion results in the elimination of the super size machine as an alternative.

7.1.3. Total Versus Incremental Returns

Continuing with the algorithm, step 5 repeats the above procedure on the next larger acceptable investment, the deluxe size machine. The results of this evaluation, the comparison of the regular and deluxe sizes, is most interesting. The incremental return on investment Δi^* for the deluxe machine exceeds the MARR. The deluxe machine is therefore "selected", as the "best" choice at this stage of the analysis.

This result is curious. How can the Deluxe machine be the best choice when it has a total return i^* that is less than the i^* of the regular machine? The following rationale is used. If I buy the regular machine and save the $120,000 difference, I earn a total of $25,000 on the regular machine plus $18,000. That is, I earn $15\% \times \$120,000$ on the alternative represented by the MARR, plus $25,000 on the regular machine, for a total of $43,000. And that total is less than the $45,000 I make on the same total investment in the deluxe machine. Thus, as noted at the start of this section, the project with the largest total return on investment may not necessarily be the best choice.

By the same logic, the deluxe machine is superior to the super-deluxe machine, as shown in the repeat of step 5 in Table 7.2. Thus, the key to this type of analysis is the recognition of the existence of the opportunity costs, and an awareness of the relationships between the total and the incremental rates of return.

7.1.4. Some Interpretations

In mutually exclusive alternatives, such as the different sizes of machines used in the above example, the larger size of investment can be considered to "economically" include the preceding acceptable alternative [1, 2]. For example, the total return on investment of the deluxe machine can be viewed as consisting of two components: the total return on investment of the regular machine plus the incremental return on the difference. Numerically, this is:

Deluxe $i^* = (25\% \times \$100,000) + (16.7\% \times \$120,000) = \$45,000.$

This is better than the regular machine and MARR combination use of the same $220,000 total investment, which yields:

$(25\% \times \$100,000) + (15\% \times \$120,000) = \$43,000.$

This example illustrates two major points. First, it is clearly *not correct* to select the investment with the largest total return on investment. Secondly, rationing of capital through arbitrary budget limits can lead to serious suboptimization. For example, suppose an absolute ceiling budget is set at $210,000. Then the only decision is to buy the regular machine and save the $110,000 balance. A much better return is achieved by spending slightly more money, another $10,000, and purchasing the delux machine.

Large organizations typically set expenditure ceilings and budgets apart from a consideration of the needs and alternative investment opportunities that may arise throughout the budgetary period. For example, many annual research, development, engineering, and capital budgets are set as a percentage of last year's sales. The organization may never look beyond these limits for the existence of additional opportunities, e.g., a deluxe size machine might never be considered if the budget were set at $200,000.

7.2. RETIREMENT/REPLACEMENT OF AGING EQUIPMENT

The decision to retire (take a machine out of production without replacing it) or replace operating equipment involves a comparison of mutually exclusive alternative cost streams. As operating equipment ages, the usual pattern is for its capital costs to decline and its operating costs to rise. When summed, these two cost functions result in a U-shaped total cost curve. Whether or not the equipment should be retired and replaced at the lowest point on this curve (or at some other point) depends upon the available alternatives and their cost profiles. Two questions need to be answered: Should the equipment be replaced now or later? How long should the new machine be kept?

7.2.1. Example: Replacing an Old Machine

Consider the example shown in Table 7.3. The first step in analyzing a retirement-replacement decision is to compute the equivalent uniform annual cost path for retaining the old machine. The equivalent

Table 7.3. Retirement/Replacement Example.

$\text{MARR} = 15\%$

Current Machine Data
Original Cost = $3,000; Age = 4 years old

PAST OPERATING COSTS		EXPECTED FUTURE OPERATING COSTS	
FOR YEAR	COST	FOR YEAR	COST
1	$ 88	5	$1,128
2	182	6	1,353
3	565	7	1,678
4	940	8	1,905

SALVAGE VALUES

Now = $1,100; 1 year hence = $900; 2 years hence = $800

REPLACEMENT MACHINE DATA

Original Cost = $3,820
Annual operating costs same as old machine, except new machine reduces them by $150 per year as a result of automation.

SALVAGE VALUES

AGE	VALUE
3 years old	$1,500
4 years old	1,100
5 years old	900

annual cost of retaining the machine one more year (5 year machine life) is:

$$A_{(+1)} = (\$1,100 - \$900)\left(\frac{(0.15)(1.15)^1}{(1.15)^1 - 1}\right) + \$900(0.15) = \$365 \quad (7.1)$$

Add: Expected future operating costs $= \$1,128$

EUAC for operating old machine one more year $= \$1,493$

Note that equation (6.20) from Chapter 6 is being used to compute the $A_{(+1)}$ value. Also note especially that both the original cost of the old machine and the first four years' operating costs are irrelevant for this incremental (keep the machine one more year) decision format. They are "sunk costs" that bear no relevance whatsoever to this particular decision.

If the old machine is kept two more years, the EUAC is:

$$A_{(+2)} = (\$1,100 - \$800)\left(\frac{(0.15)(1.15)^2}{(1.15)^2 - 1}\right) + \$800(0.15) = \$304$$

Add: Expected future operating costs

$$= \$1,128 + (\$1,353 - \$1,128)\left(\frac{1}{(1.15)^2}\right)\left(\frac{(0.15)(1.15)^2}{(1.15)^2 - 1}\right) \quad (7.2)$$

$$= \$1,232$$

EUAC for operating old machine two more years $= \$1,536$.

Note the computation of the expected future operating costs. The $1,128 figure has been "included" in the $1,353 figure. Thus, for the second year, only the incremental cost needs to be dealt with. In the above calculation, the P/F factor equivalences the increment in year $+2$ to a present value, and the A/P factor annualizes it. The resulting $1,232 amount is the equivalent annual cost of $1,128 for two years plus an additional $225 in the second year.

Additional computations confirm that the EUAC values continue to rise as the machine is retained for additional years. This indicates that the low point on the EUAC path has already been reached for the now 4-year old machine, and that it should be replaced now.

7.2.2. Optimum Life of Replacement

The second step in a replacement analysis is to ascertain the optimum life of the replacement machine. For a three year horizon, the EUAC on the new machine is:

$$A = (\$3,820 - \$1,500)\left(\frac{(0.15)(1.15)^3}{(1.15)^3 - 1}\right) + \$1,500(0.15) = \$1,241$$

$$Add: \text{ Expected future operating costs} = \left[\$88\left(\frac{1}{(1.15)}\right)\right. \tag{7.3}$$

$$\left. + \$182\left(\frac{1}{(1.15)^2}\right) + \$565\left(\frac{1}{(1.15)^3}\right)\right]$$

$$\times \left(\frac{(0.15)(1.15)^3}{(1.15)^3 - 1}\right) = \$256$$

$$Minus: \$150 \text{ differential for automation} = -\$150$$

EUAC for operating the new machine for three years = \$1,347.

Additional computations show that the EUAC for keeping the new machine 4 years is \$1,361, and for 5 years is \$1,391. Thus, as Table 7.4 shows, even if the new machine is bought now and kept for 3 more

Table 7.4. EUAC Values.

+x MORE YEARS x =	EUAC IF OLD MACHINE IS KEPT EUAC	+x YEARS x =	EUAC IF OLD MACHINE IS REPLACED NOW AND NEW MACHINE IS KEPT EUAC
1	$1,493	1	$1,347
2	$1,536	2	$1,361
		3	$1,391

years, this is a better policy (EUAC = $1,391) than operating the old machine even one more year (EUAC = $1,493). Note that equations (7.2) and (7.3) are algebraically equivalent forms. The two forms illustrate the algebraic options that may be applied.

7.3. INDEPENDENT CAPITAL PROJECTS[2]

When the proposals are independent, the problem is to select the best *portfolio* of projects. And Δi^* is now computed differently than it was in the case of mutually exclusive projects (Table 7.1). Specifically, in the case of independent projects, the IRR values are the incremental returns, that is, IRR $= \Delta i^*$. This is because the projects are *independent*. The next larger investment represents a whole new project, not just a more expensive version that "contains" the prior version [1].

7.3.1. Algorithm for Independent Projects

For independent projects, a *classical capital budgeting approach* is often taken. This approach consists of the following steps [1]:

First, eliminate any proposals whose IRR value is less than the MARR. Second, array the projects in order of descending values of the IRR. Third, select projects into the portfolio in decreasing IRR values until the budget is exhausted.

7.3.2. An Example

To illustrate the above algorithm, assume the projects in Table 7.2 had been independent proposals. With a budget of $100,000, the best portfolio is to select only the regular size machine. With a budget of $350,000, the best portfolio is the regular size plus the deluxe size, plus saving the $30,000 balance (investing it in the 15% MARR alternative); and so forth. Note that the economy size is eliminated from any consideration because its IRR < the MARR of 15%.

Some decision makers would be inclined to reason that the economy size could be included where there are enough high return projects to offset it, so that the total return on investment is above the MARR.

---

[2] The examples herein are based on the author's case studies in References 1 and 2, reprinted by permission.

This is incorrect economic logic. For example, a budget of $370,000 permits the selection of a portfolio of the economy size plus the regular size plus the deluxe size, for a total portfolio return of $75,000 on the $370,000 investment. But, if instead, the $50,000 spent on the economy size is saved at the MARR rate, the total return is $2,500 more on the same total investment.

On the other hand, there may be irreducible reasons for including the economy size in the portfolio and thereby incurring the $2,500 opportunity cost, e.g., the economy size may provide a balanced capability for the plant. But the decision maker should be aware of the economic cost of such irreducibles, as a basis for deciding whether or not to incur these costs. Economic analysis computations are thus often helpful for elucidating such costs.

7.4. ZERO-ONE PROJECTS

Zero-one type projects are a particular type of independent project. In the zero-one case, each alternative project is either rejected completely (the "zero" case) or selected and funded at some pre-budgeted level (the "one" case). Table 7.5 presents an algorithm for zero-one projects [1].

To illustrate the zero-one projects case, let us use the data shown in Table 7.6. Let us define $V = P/I$ as the value of a project. Following the algorithm, the alternative with the largest V number is selected first. This is project 5. Continue the iterations (continue performing steps 1 and 2 of the algorithm) on the next best alternative, and so forth, until the budget is exhausted. The results are shown in Table 7.7. The "Increase in $\sum V$" column of Table 7.7 shows the incremental change in the total value of the portfolio for each incremental expenditure. This column reflects the effects of selecting the best alternative first [1].

7.5. OPTIMUM BUDGET DETERMINATION

Based on the results in Table 7.7, the wisdom of a $6,000,000 budget may now be questioned. In fact, this budget may be too large. A $3,500,000 budget may be more nearly optimal. Beyond the $3,500,000 point (iteration 3 in Table 7.7), the incremental value per dollar expended falls off rapidly. This is shown by the data in the "Increase in $\sum V$" column of Table 7.7.

Table 7.5. Algorithm for Analyzing Zero One Proposals.

STEP	ACTION OR DECISION
1	Rank the decision alternatives in decreasing order of their value. Alternatives with the same ranking (ties) may be listed in any order.
2	Select the highest-ranked alternative. If ties exist, select the highest ranked alternative with the lowest cost. Remove this selected alternative from the list of candidates and place it in the set of funded alternatives.
3	Subtract the cost of this selected alternative from the available funds. If the available funds are inadequate for this selected alternative, then replace it in the candidate list and select the next best alternative that can be funded with the available funds.
4	Iterate (continue performing) steps 2 and 3 until the available funds or the budget is exhausted. If funds remain after funding all the alternatives, or if the remaining alternatives each cost more than the available funds, then these funds are simply left over.

Table 7.6. Five Alternative Zero-One Projects.

BUDGET = $6,000,000

	PRESENT WORTH EXPECTED PROFITS, P	PRESENT WORTH INVESTMENT, I	$V = P/I$
Project 1	$35M	$2,500,000	14
Project 2	5M	1,000,000	5
Project 3	10M	500,000	20
Project 4	40M	2,000,000	20
Project 5	28M	1,000,000	28

Table 7.7. Results From the Algorithm.

ITERATION NUMBER	RESULTING PORTFOLIO	$\sum I$	$\sum P$	$\sum V$	INCREASE IN $\sum V$
1	Project 5	$1,000,000	$28M	28	28
2	Project 5 + Project 3	$1,500,000	$38M	48	20
3	Project 5 + Project 3 + Project 4	$3,500,000	$78M	68	20
4	Project 5 + Project 3 + Project 4 + Project 1 Budget is exhausted	$6,000,000	$113M	82	14

Of course, if there are no better alternatives, then it may be reasonable to go on to iteration 4 and spend the additional $2,500,000 on projects 4 and 1. However, if the $2,500,000 can be spent elsewhere to achieve more than $V = 14$, then it should indeed be spent elsewhere [1].

This is precisely the logic of using the MARR as a cutoff rate. For instance, if an MARR had been set, and if $14\% <$ MARR $< 20\%$, then the optimum portfolio would consist of projects 5, 3, and 4, and the optimum budget would be $3,500,000. Similarly, if $20\% <$ MARR $< 28\%$ then the optimum portfolio would consist of only project 5 and the optimum budget could be $1,000,000.

7.5.1. Suboptimal Budget Constraints

The more common situation, of course, is the case where the budget has been set too low [1]. Table 7.8 illustrates a case where the total budget has been set so low that it adversely constrains the contributions. The difference between the purchasing power of this $2,500,000 budget and a $3,500,000 budget can be seen by comparing the data in Tables 7.7 and 7.8. For the additional $4,000,000 difference between the $2,500,000 budget in Table 7.8 and a $3,500,000 budget (see Table 7.7), there is an additional increase in $\sum P$ from $43M to $78M. That is, the incremental value-contribution rate is ($78M $-$ $43M)/$1,000,000 $= 35$. This is higher than the contribution rate (the V number) for any of the alternatives in Table 7.7. How can this be? The answer is that the $2,500,000 budget is a *very* uneconomical one. From Table 7.8 we can see that the economically questionable project

Table 7.8. Results Under A Budget of $2,500,000.

ITERATION NUMBER	PORTFOLIO	$\sum I$	$\sum P$	INCREASE IN $\sum V$
1	Project 5	$1,000,000	$28M	28
2	Project 5 Project 3	$1,500,000	$38M	20
3	Project 5 Project 3 Project 2 Budget is exhausted	$2,500,000	$43M	5

2 (see Table 7.6) was funded at the last iteration. Why? Because there was no other alternative use for the $1,000,000 which remained at the end of iteration 2, the algorithm brought project 2 into the portfolio. If the total budget had been $3,500,000, the algorithm would *not* have selected project 2. Rather, it would have selected the economically superior alternative 4. This is precisely what happened in Table 7.7. Thus, it is the suboptimal $2,500,000 budget that severely constrains the results in Table 7.8.

Suboptimal budgets can also exist in the case of mutually exclusive projects [1]. For example, let us return to Table 7.2. With the MARR = 15%, the optimum budget becomes $220,000. There is no point in setting the budget at $250,000. It becomes redundant. On the other hand, if the budget had been set at $200,000 with the MARR = 15%, there would have been a conflict between the budget and the MARR. The MARR would have directed us to select the deluxe machine. But the $200,000 budget and the 15% MARR *together* would have constrained us to select the regular machine, thus only spending $100,000 of the $200,000 budget and "investing" the remainder in the MARR. In this case, then, the two constraints, the $200,000 budget and the 15% MARR are inconsistent. If the MARR is correctly set, then the budget is too low. If the budget is correctly set, then the MARR is redundant [1].

7.5.2. Avoiding Suboptimal Budgets and Redundant Constraints

Suboptimal budgets and contradictory or inconsistent constraints are common in organizational settings. Budgets and return criteria are often set for long range planning purposes, in isolation from a careful analysis of the available projects and investment alternatives. Moreover, optimal budgets and criteria can become nonoptimal over time. Unexpected new projects and opportunities often appear on the scene. And the premises and information on which the budgets and criteria were originally based can easily change over time. The above methods can be especially useful for specifying optimal budgets and criteria, for examining their appropriateness over time, and for readjusting them to take new information and changed circumstances into account [1].

7.6. INCLUDING DEPRECIATION IN THE ANALYSES[3]

Depreciation is a way of accounting for the original cost of an asset over its useful life. In effect, it is an attempt to apportion the prepaid cost of a bundle of services over the period in which those services are used. The purchase of an asset represents a prepayment for a bundle of future services. Depreciation amortizes this prepayment over the life of the asset, so as to obtain a more perfect matching of the cost of the asset with the time period of actual use of these services.

The annual amount of the asset's cost that is charged off for depreciation is called the *annual depreciation*. The running total of the annual depreciation amounts is the *accumulated depreciation*. The accumulated depreciation is normally reported at the end of each year, as part of the firm's annual accounting practices. The running total of the undepreciated or unamortized portion of the asset's *original cost* is the asset's *book value*. The book value is also normally reported at the end of each year, as part of the annual accounting practices. The *original cost* of an asset is the amount paid for it, including delivery and installation costs.

The *salvage value* of an asset is determined at the time the asset is purchased, and is an estimate of the proceeds that will be realized from the sale or other disposition of the asset when it is retired. If the asset is retired at the end of its useful life, then the salvage value will often be equal to the scrap price. Otherwise, the salvage value may be higher than the scrap value, and equal to the going market price for a used asset of this type. The *net salvage* value is the salvage value minus the cost of removing the asset from the premises. For some types of machinery, the cost of removal, unhooking peripheral equipment, dismantling it for removal, etc. may be significant. However, when the cost of removal exceeds the salvage value, the net salvage value is zero. A negative net salvage value is not currently allowed by the U.S. Internal Revenue Service regulations in computing annual depreciation.[4]

The *adjusted cost* of an asset is its original cost less its salvage value. Either the net salvage value or the salvage value may be used in determining the adjusted cost for tax purposes, according to current tax laws.[4]

---

[3] This section is based on the author's discussion and examples which are presented in Reference 2, reprinted by permission.
[4] Tax regulations change; the latest tax laws should always be consulted.

The *useful life* of an asset is the time period over which it will be depreciated. The useful life of an asset may or may not be the same as its service life, physical life, economic life, or market life. Current U.S. tax laws state that the useful life of an asset depends upon the frequency of use of the asset, its age when acquired, how frequently it is repaired and maintained, its rate of technological obsolescence, and other factors. The U.S. Treasury Department provides useful life guidelines for an extensive list of common assets. Anyone wishing to use a different useful life than the Treasury's guidelines may request a special determination from the U.S. Internal Revenue Service Department.[5] The useful life, original cost and salvage value of the asset are the key elements in determining its depreciation [1, 2].

7.6.1. Four Methods of Depreciation

Four commonly used methods of calculating annual depreciation are: the percent usage method, the straight line method, the declining balance method, and the sum-of-years-digits method. The annual percentage usage method charges off a pro-rata percentage of the original cost of the maching, i.e.,

$$\frac{\text{This year's}}{\text{depreciation}} = \left(\begin{array}{c}\text{Original}\\\text{cost}\end{array}\right) \times \left(\frac{\text{Volume produced}}{\text{this year}}\middle/\frac{}{\text{Total life volume}}\right) \times 100\%$$

Note that, unlike the other three methods, this method makes no provision for salvage values. Because the other methods have a greater tax advantage, this method is not widely used.

The straight line (SL) method is:

$$\text{Annual Depreciation} = \frac{(\text{Original cost}) - (\text{Salvage value})}{\text{Useful life, in years}}$$

The straight-line (SL) depreciation *rate* is given by:

$$\frac{\text{Annual depreciation}}{\text{Original cost} - \text{Salvage value}} \times 100\%$$

---

[5] The latest tax laws should always be consulted.

The SL method implicitly assumes that the amount of each year's depreciation is the same. This condition may not be representative of real annual usage conditions, and thus the SL method is often referred to as an approximate method.

In the declining balance method, a rate twice that of the straight line method is currently allowed for tax purposes.[6] Thus, this method is often called the "double-declining balance" (DDB) method. This rate is applied to the book value of the asset, rather than to its cost. For example, in the DDB method, an asset with an expected 10-year life that originally cost $10,000 would be depreciated at a 20% rate as follows:

Year	1	2	3	$\cdots$	n
Book value	$10,000	$8,000	$6,400	$\cdots$	>0
Depreciation (at the 20% rate)	$2,000	$1,600	$1,280	$\cdots$	>0

Note that the DDB method provides an earlier write-off of assets: more of the total cost is written off in earlier years.

The sum-of-years-digits is

$$S = \sum_{j=1}^{n} j = 1 + 2 + 3 + \cdots + n = \frac{n(n+1)}{2},$$

where n is the life of the asset in years. The sum-of-years-digits (SYD) depreciation charge is computed as:

$$\begin{array}{l} \text{Annual depreciation} \\ \text{charge for year } i \end{array} = \left(\frac{i}{S}\right) \times (\text{Original Cost} - \text{Salvage}).$$

Since the SYD method doesn't write off the asset quite as rapidly as the DDB method, it is less appealing for tax reasons.

7.6.2. Comparison of SL, DDB, and SYD Methods[7]

Table 7.9 presents the SL depreciation schedule for machine A. This machine has an original cost of $160,000, a useful life of 10 years, a

---

[6] Tax laws and allowable rates change frequently. The reader should check the most recent rates.

[7] Tables 7.9, 7.10, 7.11 and Figures 7.1 and 7.2 in this section are based on the author's examples presented in Reference 2, reprinted by permission.

Table 7.9. Straight Line (SL) Depreciation Schedule

YEAR	DEPRECIATION CHARGE (10%) FOR YEAR	ACCUMULATED DEPRECIATION	BOOK VALUE AT END OF YEAR
1	$15,000	$15,000	$145,000
2	15,000	30,000	130,000
3	15,000	45,000	115,000
4	15,000	60,000	100,000
5	15,000	75,000	85,000
6	15,000	90,000	70,000
7	15,000	105,000	55,000
8	15,000	120,000	40,000
9	15,000	135,000	25,000
10	15,000	150,000	10,000

salvage value of $15,000, and a cost of $5,000 for removal at the end of its useful life. Note that, as shown in Table 7.9, the SL method results in a level depreciation charge: the same depreciation charge occurs in each year of the asset's useful life. Similarly, the accumulated depreciation and book value are linear functions of the age of the asset. These are characteristics of the SL depreciation method. The $10,000 book value remaining at the end of the useful life of the asset is equal to its net scrap (salvage) value. The sale of the asset for its salvage value will remove this book value from the firm's accounting records.

Table 7.10 presents the DDB depreciation schedule for this same machine A. Note that over half of the depreciation occurs before the asset is at the halfway point in its useful life. In fact, by the end of the fifth year in the asset's ten-year life, the DDB method has charged off ($107,571.20/$142,164.76) $\times$ 100% − 76% of the total depreciation that can be taken. This is a typical pattern for the DDB method. By contrast, a comparison with the results in Table 7.9 shows that in the SL method exactly half of the total depreciation is taken during the first half of the asset's useful life. Note also that in the DDB method the book value never reaches the scrap value. Again, this is a typical result with the DDB method. The excess of the asset's end-of-life book value over its net scrap value is normally handled as a capital loss in the firm's accounting records, when the asset is sold. For instance, in Table 7.10, the difference of $17,835.24 − $10,000 = $7,835.24 will be deducted from the firm's income as a capital loss. It may be

Table 7.10. Double Declining Balance (DDB) Depreciation Schedule.

YEAR	DEPRECIATION CHARGE (20%) FOR YEAR	ACCUMULATED DEPRECIATION	BOOK VALUE AT END OF YEAR
1	$32,000	$32,000	$128,000
2	25,600	57,600	102,400
3	20,480	78,080	81,920
4	16,384	94,464	65,536
5	13,107.20	107,571.20	52,428.80
6	9,830.40	117.401.60	42,598.40
7	8,830.40	125,790.21	34,209.79
8	6,710.88	132,501.09	27,498.91
9	5,368.71	137,869.80	22,130.20
10	4,294.96	142,164.76	17,835.24

Table 7.11. Sum-of-Years-Digits (SYD) Depreciation Schedule.

YEAR	AMOUNT OF DEPRECIATION CHARGE FOR YEAR	ACCUMULATED DEPRECIATION	BOOK VALUE AT END OF YEAR
1	$27,272.73	$27,272.73	$132,727.27
2	24,545.45	51,818.18	108,181.82
3	21,818.18	73,636.36	86,363.64
4	19,090.91	92,727.27	67,272.73
5	16,363.64	109,090.91	50,909.09
6	13,636.36	122,727.27	37,272.73
7	10,909.09	133,636.36	26,363.64
8	8,181.82	141,818.18	18,181.82
9	5,454.55	147,272.73	12,727.27
10	2,727.27	150,000.00	10,000.00

noted here that current tax laws[8] do not permit the accumulated depreciation to ever exceed the adjusted cost of the asset, thus keeping a firm from depreciating an asset below its salvage value. Hence, in the DDB method, if the book value of the asset ever drops to the level of the asset's salvage value, then its depreciable life is over.

Table 7.11 presents the SYD depreciation schedule for machine A. Note, as the data in Table 7.11 show, a different amount of depreciation is charged off each year.

---

[8] Tax laws change, and the most recent laws should always be checked.

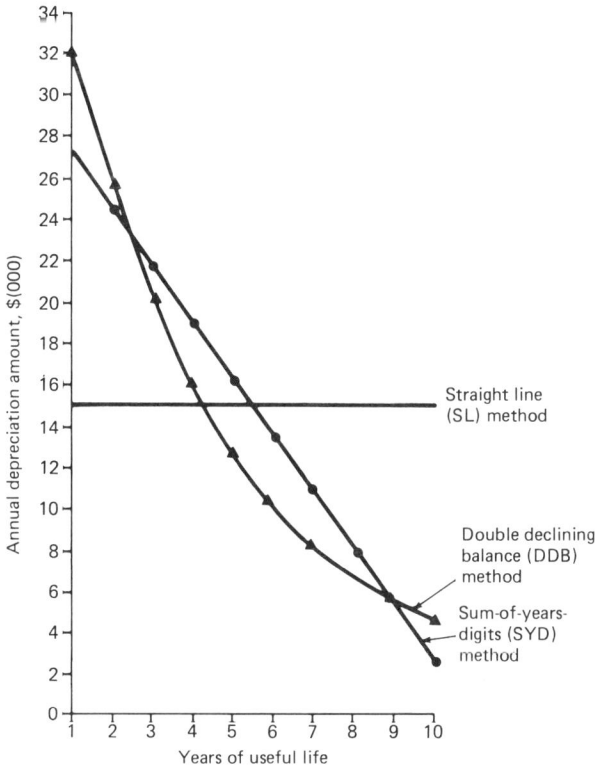

Figure 7.1.

Figures 7.1 and 7.2 are plots of the annual depreciation charges and book values from Tables 7.9, 7.10, and 7.11. As Figure 7.1 shows, the sum-of-the-years-digits (SYD) and double declining balance (DDB) methods are forms of accelerated depreciation. They generate a pattern of decreasing depreciation charges over the life of the asset. In these methods, most of the asset's depreciation occurs during the earlier portion of the asset's useful life. By comparison in Figure 7.1, the straight line (SL) method generates neither an increasing or decreasing pattern. It distributes the asset's depreciation evenly over its useful life.

As Figure 7.2 shows, each method generates a different pattern of book values over the useful life of the asset. The SYD and DDB methods generate the lowest book values. Note how the book value at the end of the 10th year in the DDB method is above the salvage

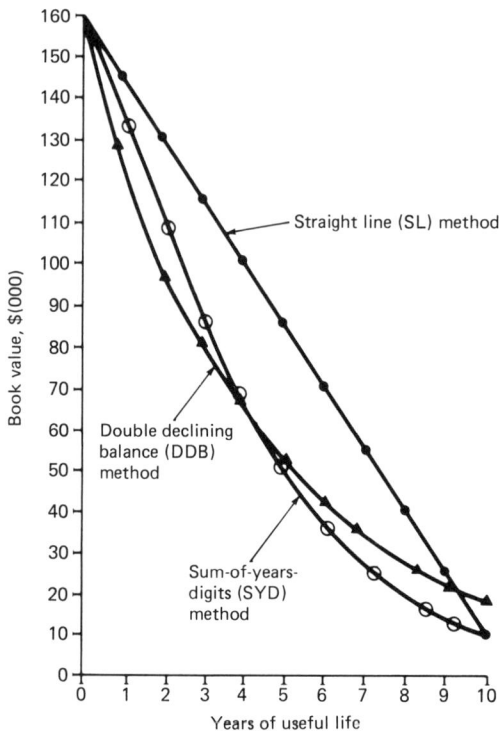

Figure 7.2.

value of the asset, as discussed above. For more details the reader is referred to References 1 and 2.

7.6.3. Effects of Depreciation

Because depreciation is deducted in determining business net income, it effectively lowers the taxes the business would otherwise pay. Specifically, if the normal tax rate is t, then the *depreciation tax shield* or amount of taxes saved due to depreciation is given by

$$S_j = t_r \times D_j$$

where S_j is the tax savings in the jth year and D_j is the depreciation charge for that year.

Over the life of an asset, the total amount of depreciation tax shield will be the same with the straight line and sum-of-years-digits method. However, because of the time value of money, accelerated depreciation methods like the sum-of-years-digits and the double declining balance methods have a decided advantage over the straight-line method. In general, accelerated depreciation methods will yield a larger present worth net income after taxes. This is because the accelerated methods provide a larger tax shield in the earlier years of the asset's life, thus increasing the after tax net income in these years. Since money has a time value, these early savings also have a value.

In general, either the double declining balance or the sum-of-years-digits methods will usually be the most advantageous to use. The choice of one method over the other should be made on the basis of the current tax laws and the results and consequences of each method. Figures like 7.1 and 7.2 are often helpful in making this choice.

7.6.4. Impact of Depreciation

The influence of depreciation is easily seen from the following example: a machine that costs $50,000 has a life of 12 years and will provide a $12,000 savings in annual operating costs. The return on investment before taxes without depreciation is:

$$0 = -\$50,000 + \$12,000\left(\frac{(1 + i)^{10} - 1}{(i)(1 + i)^{10}}\right) \qquad (7.4)$$

$$i^* = 20.3\%.$$

The return on investment after taxes, assuming a tax rate[9] of 51%, without depreciation is:

$$0 = -\$50,000 + \$5,880\left(\frac{(1 + i)^{10} - 1}{(i)(1 + i)^{10}}\right) \qquad (7.5)$$

$$i^* = 3\%.$$

---

[9] Tax rates may vary, and the reader is advised to check the current tax rates.

The return on investment after taxes, using straight-line depreciation, is computed as follows:

Before tax savings	$ 12,000
Depreciation	− 5,000
Before tax income	$ 7,000
Taxes at 51%	− 3,570
After tax income	$ 3,430

Since depreciation is an accounting entry which takes no cash, the
true cash flow here is $3,430 + $5,000 = $8,430. Thus, the return on
investment is:

$$0 = -\$50,000 + \$8,430\left(\frac{(1 + i)^{10} - 1}{(i)(1 + i)^{10}}\right) \tag{7.6}$$

$$i^* = 10.9\%$$

A good rule to follow is to make all economic calculations on an
after-tax basis. This will take into account any depreciation-related
differential cash flows that might exist between two competing alternatives, e.g., where one of the alternatives has a shorter lifetime. It is
quite possible for two alternatives to reverse their order of preference
as one goes from a before-tax to an after-tax calculation [2].

7.7. INCORPORATING RISK ASSESSMENTS IN THE ANALYSES

Probabilities can be incorporated into most economic appraisal calculations to discount the data for riskiness. The most typical method
is to compute expected values, i.e., multiply the probability times the
cash flow, the cost, etc. For instance, suppose it has been estimated
that there is a 0.60 likelihood that the machine referred to in Section
7.6.4 above will actually yield $12,000 in before-tax savings. Then,
equation (7.6) becomes:

$$0 = -\$50,000 + (0.60) \times (\$8,430)\left(\frac{(1 + i)^{10} - 1}{(i)(1 + i)^{10}}\right).$$

If the most likely, optimistic and pessimistic values of the variables can be estimated, then a confidence analysis can be made. In this analysis, a β-distribution is fitted to the most likely, optimistic, and pessimistic values to derive statistical confidence estimates. The mean of the β-distribution, E, is given by:

$$E = \frac{O + 4M + P}{6},$$

where O = the optimistic case, M = the most likely case, and P = the pessimistic estimate. For this approximation to be a good one, O and P must be the "1 in a 100" occurrences. The standard deviation, σ, of the β-distribution is approximated by

$$\sigma = \left(\frac{P - O}{6}\right)$$

Then, the 95% confidence limits are $E \pm 2\sigma$. As an example, suppose we have the following EUAC data:

EUAC Values

	O	M	P	E	σ
Machine 1	$400	$1,000	$5,000	$1,567	$767
Machine 2	500	2,000	2,500	1,833	333

Let us assume the project manager has an equipment budget of $2,500 and that he can buy either of two machines for the $2,500. Now, on the basis of the most likely values (the M values), Machine 1 is preferred to Machine 2. But on a 95% confidence analysis:

$$EUAC_1 = \$1,567 + (2 \times \$767) = \$3,101$$

$$EUAC_2 = \$1,833 + (2 \times \$333) = \$2,499.$$

Thus, if the project manager wishes to be 95% confident of not exceeding his budget, he must choose machine 2. Yet, machine 2 is the one with the higher M value (cost)!

This example is, of course, contrived. But it is not unrepresentative of the types of reversals that can actually occur. The above type of analysis thus provides the manager with a more complete picture of the apparent risks in the alternatives. It results in an improved information base which a manager can use to contemplate the relative merits of the $2,500 budget and the trade-offs between the two alternative machines [1, 2, 3].

7.8. HANDLING INFLATION

An allowance for inflation may be made in the interest rate used in economic appraisal calculations (see Chapter 6, Section 6.3.6). Inflation may also be accounted for in two other useful ways: by appropriately increasing the MARR and by indexing the dollar amounts. Table 7.12 provides an illustration of this.

Column 2 of Table 7.12 gives the NPV for Project A without any account being taken of the inflation rate. Project A shows a positive NPV. Hence, Project A is acceptable. Column 3 gives the NPV data and results where $i = $ MARR + inflation rate = 10% + 5% = 15%. In this case, the NPV is negative. Hence, Project A is not acceptable. Equivalent results are achieved if the cash flows are first indexed and then multiplied by the (P/F) factor, as shown in column 5 of Table 7.12. Thus, if inflation is taken into account, the decision is reversed: the previously acceptable Project A becomes unacceptable.

The sensitivity of any decision to reversal, as shown here, should always be tested by either the $i = $ MARR + inflation rate method or

Table 7.12. Comparison of Methods for Handling Inflation on Project A.

MARR $= 10\%$; INFLATION RATE $= 5\%$

YEAR $n =$	COLUMN 1: CASH FLOWS	COLUMN 2: PW $@i = 10\%$	COLUMN 3: PW $@i = 15\%$	COLUMN 4: INDEXED VALUES*	COLUMN 5: COLUMN 4 $\times (P/F)$
0	$-$10,000	$-$10,000	$-$10,000	$-$10,000	$-$10,000
1	$+$3,000	$+$2,727	$+$2,600	$+$2,860	$+$2,600
2	$+$4,000	$+$3,304	$+$2,990	$+$3,620	$+$2,990
3	$+$6,000	$+$4,506	$+$3,880	$+$5,180	$+$3,880
	NPV $=$	$+$537	$-$530		$-$530

*Column 1 item $\div (1.05)^n$.

the indexed values method. It may be that the results will be found insensitive to a wide variation in the inflation rate, i.e., there is no reversal in the rank ordering of the alternatives. In the latter case, the analysis will assure the decision maker that he need not be concerned about purchasing the "wrong" machine if the inflation rate changes [2, 3].

7.9. SUMMARY AND CONCLUSIONS

This chapter has reviewed the applications of economic appraisal methods to project selection. Economic appraisal methods deal with the economic and monetary aspects of project selection decision making. They focus on the costs and economic benefits, with the aim of clarifying which project(s) are economically best.

Economic appraisal methods depend on several economic concepts, including the concept of opportunity costs, incremental values and costs, equivalency, and the time value of money. Economic appraisal techniques include the equivalent uniform annual cost (EUAC) model, the present value or present worth (PW) model, the internal rate of return (IRR) model, the net present value (NPV) model, and the payback period (PBP) model presented in Chapter 6. Applications of these models may include equipment purchases, minimum cost problems, retirement/replacement of equipment, analysis of capital investment and expansion problems, determination of optimum budgets and investment levels, and the analysis of return on investments. Some of these applications have been reviewed and illustrated in this chapter.

Where sufficient data and information are available, economic appraisal methods should be used as aids to project selection decision making. However, in most cases, only certain portions of the decision problem can be reduced to economic criteria and monetary terms. Many irreducibles will usually remain. Economic appraisal methods can thus only serve as aids to decision making, helping to reduce and systematize the volume of information, and assisting with the structuring of the problem. Experienced judgment, wisdom, and decision making competency are thus central to effective project selection decision making. Economic appraisal methods should be viewed as ways to enhance these qualities.

7.10. REFERENCES

1. Souder, W. E. *Management Decision Methods for Managers of Engineering and Research.* New York: Van Nostrand Reinhold, 1980, pp. 100–134.
2. Gottfried, B. G. and W. E. Souder. *Engineering Economy.* New York: McGraw-Hill, 1983.
3. Canada, J. R. *Intermediate Economic Analysis for Management and Engineering.* New Jersey: Prentice-Hall, 1971, pp. 171–392.

8. Project Monitoring, Termination, and Reselection

8.0. PROJECT SELECTION FOLLOW-UP

Once a project is selected and work on it has been initiated, the entire project effort must be carefully monitored during its life cycle. Costs and schedules in a project proposal are estimates, and significant variances may be encountered in the outcome of the project. Moreover, there are numerous events and external forces that may emerge to influence the outcome of the project. These forces may cause the project to go astray unless it is carefully watched. The project may even have to be replanned or modified as a result of these forces and influences. Such aspects are part of the project appraisal and selection system, since they may influence the established project portfolio and budget allocations. Even minor changes in one project may start a chain of events that creates the need to readjust the entire portfolio, select one or more new projects, and/or reallocate the established budgets.

Completed projects create both opportunities and burdens that influence project selection decisions. A completed project releases resources and provides an opportunity to select another project and initiate work on it. But a completed project often places a burden on the performing group to make sure that their outputs and results are properly transferred to the successor department. For example, research personnel are seldom immediately freed at the end of a research project. Rather, they are often occupied for several months in writing reports, training new personnel, and performing general technology transfer activities aimed at making sure their work is properly transferred to the development group. These transfer activities influence the timing of the selection and initiation of the subsequent research project. In some cases, these delays may penalize the subsequent project, e.g., the delay may cause the subsequent project to overrun its targeted completion date.

Delaying the termination of an unsuccessful project can also have a significant effect on the project selection process. Delaying a termination decision creates opportunity costs in committed resources which could be used elsewhere, and delays other project selection decisions.

In this chapter, several techniques and methods are presented for project monitoring, for handling project completions, and for making timely project termination decisions. The interrelationships between these aspects and project appraisal/selection are discussed.

8.1. PROJECT MONITORING

A project is appraised and selected on the basis of a particular set of information. Any changes in this set of information over time may affect the relative cost and value of that project, vis-à-vis the other projects and alternatives. Thus, any and all changes over time must be monitored and assessed. Adjustments in the previous project selection decision, or entirely new project selection decisions, may be required.

8.2. COST-PROGRESS MONITORING[1]

The cost-progress approach gives a detailed, complete tracking of the behavior of the project over its life cycle. Expenditure rates per time and achievements per time period are integrated in a system that permits early indications of pending overruns.

8.2.1. The Cost-Progress Model

To illustrate the cost-progress approach let t be the time period, $t = 1, 2, \ldots, n$. Let E_t be the cumulative dollars actually expended by the end of time period t. Let E_t^* be the cumulative dollars forecasted to be expended by the end of time period t. Then, let $\Delta E_t =$

---

[1] This section is based on W. E. Souder, *Management Decision Methods for Managers of Engineering and Research*. New York: Van Nostrand Reinhold, 1980, pp. 308–311, by permission.

$(F_i^* - F_i)$ = the cost variance for t. Let ϕ_t be the cumulative actual output at the end of time period t, and ϕ_t^* = the cumulative forecasted output at the end of time period t, and $\Delta\phi_t = (\phi_t - \phi_t^*)$ be the progress variance for t. Let C_t^* be the total *forecasted* cost of the total *actual* output at the end of t, and let $\Delta C_t = (C_t^* - E_t)$ be the cost-progress variance for t. The outputs, ϕ_t and ϕ_t^*, may be measured in terms of milestones, the percentage of the nodes completed in a PERT or CPM network plan, or other measures [1, 2]. The variances ΔE_t, $\Delta\phi_t$, and ΔC_t are the information feedbacks that monitor costs and achievements over time. When these variances become large enough, they should trigger a reallocation of resources, the replanning of the project, the reselection of new projects, etc.

8.2.2. An Example of Cost-Progress Measurement

These ideas are illustrated in Table 8.1 and Figure 8.1. To visualize how this model functions, suppose that at the end of time period 5 the actual output has been determined to be 0.40 (40% of the project milestones have been achieved) and the total actual amount expended has been determined to be \$100,000. Therefore, a mark X_5 was made at the coordinates $E = 100$ and $\phi = 0.4$ in Figure 8.1, ignoring for the moment the time scale. The appropriate values of the parameters E_t^*, E_t, ϕ_t^*, ϕ_t, and C_t^* were entered in the analysis of budget variance table shown in Table 8.1, and the respective variances were computed.

Likewise, the marks X_1, X_2, X_3, ..., X_8 were made in Figure 8.1 for months 1, 2, 3, ..., 8 and the corresponding variances were

Table 8.1. Analysis of Budget Variance Table.

	EXPENDITURE			OUTPUT			COST/PROGRESS	
t	E_t	E_t^*	ΔE_t	ϕ_t	ϕ_t^*	$\Delta\phi_t$	C_t^*	ΔC_t
1	20	20	0	0.10	0.10	0	20	0
2	50	40	-10	0.25	0.15	$+0.10$	75	$+25$
3	60	70	$+10$	0.35	0.25	$+0.10$	85	$+25$
4	75	90	$+15$	0.40	0.40	0	90	$+15$
5	100	120	$+20$	0.40	0.65	-0.25	90	-10
6	130	140	$+10$	0.70	0.75	-0.05	130	0
7	180	160	-20	0.70	0.85	-0.15	130	-50
8	230	180	-50	0.70	0.87	-0.17	130	-100

similarly computed and entered in Table 8.1. Note that the forecast line in Figure 8.1 is simply a graphic portrayal of the project plan.

This model enables management to see variances as they occur, categorize their causes and determine the appropriate response to be taken. For example, the data in Table 8.1 and Figure 8.1 show that the manager should not be concerned about the overspending indicated by the negative cost variance at the end of the second month ($\Delta E_2 = -10$). The cost-progress variance is positive ($\Delta C_2 = +25$), indicating that the extra expenditure has "bought" more than proportionate achievements. Note the location of X_2 in Figure 8.1. In other words, running over budget will not matter if the overexpenditure is "buying" proportionate achievements. But, now consider the data for the third, fourth, and fifth months in Table 8.1 and Figure 8.1. The absolute level of achievement is slipping at an increasing rate, as shown by the entries in the $\Delta \phi_t$ column changing from $+0.10$, through 0, to -0.25. And the level of achievement per amount of expenditure is also slipping, as shown by the entries in the ΔC_t column.

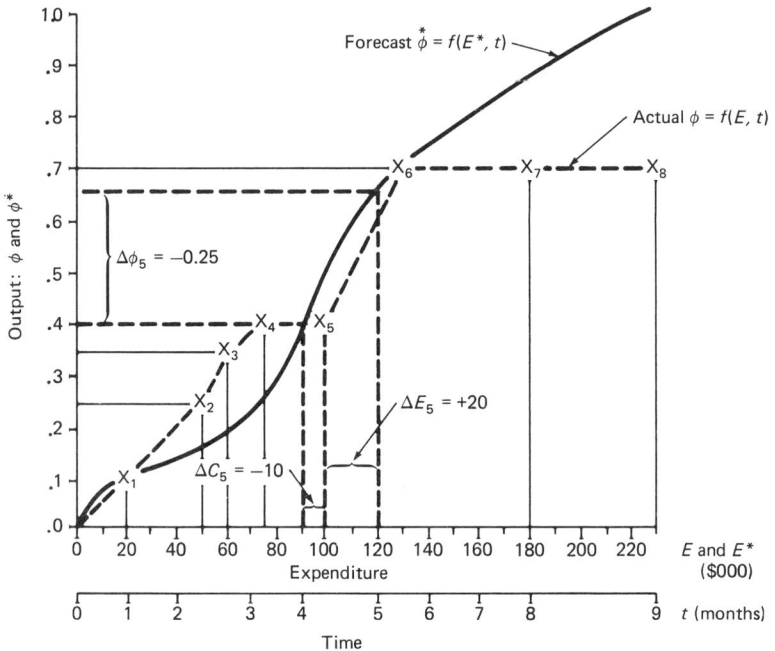

Figure 8.1. Cost-progress control model example.

Not only is the project achieving less with each passing month, but it is also achieving less per dollar with each passing month. But none of this bad news shows in the budget or cost variance (the ΔE_t column in Table 8.1). In fact, the project shows a favorable status in budgetary control (positive entries in the ΔE_t column) over these three months.

8.2.3. Interpreting the Variances

The conclusion is that controlling by budget overruns and underruns *only* can be seriously misleading. Cost (or budget) variances and achievement variances can balance out, as shown at the end of the sixth month in Table 8.1 and Figure 8.1. Or they may reinforce each other, as shown at the end of months seven and eight in Table 8.1. In any event, it is the *interaction* of both the cost and achievement variances that determines the actual status of the project.

This simple fact is often obscured in many monitoring situations. As a result, an inordinate amount of significance is generally attached to project cost overruns, while some projects running under their budgeted costs often fail to attract badly needed attention. For example, even under fixed manpower assignments, misalignments may occur because a manager may choose to underconsume a fair share of outside services, e.g., analytical services, in the interest of staying under budget. Or the manager may underconsume in the hope of reserving some funds for other projects. The cost-progress approach makes the effects of such misalignments immediately apparent. Thus, projects that are running cost-progress variances are candidates for replanning, reappraisal or termination [1, 2].

8.3. ENVIRONMENTAL MONITORING

A desired product can quickly become a "no longer needed" product in the face of changing markets, the advent of a competing product or a substitute item, the emergence of a radical new technology, or the advent of new laws and regulations. Thus, a project that appeared to be a winner when it was selected can become a loser during the time it is being worked on, through no fault of its own. Changes in the external environment can change the cost, benefit, risk, and suitability characteristics of the project—the bases on which it was originally selected. If the bases change, the project may no longer be viable.

Table 8.2. Five Environmental Areas to be Monitored.

Technological
User needs/wants
Markets
Competition
Socio-legal

And consideration should thus be given to redesigning the ideas, reprioritizing the project, rescheduling the work, reallocating the funds, backlogging the effort, or terminating the project and selecting a replacement project.

The project environment should be monitored with respect to five major areas. These areas are listed in Table 8.2, and discussed below.

8.3.1. Technological

New technologies that may impact the current project are usually not difficult to monitor. The technical and professional personnel will often keep up to date on new patents and new developments in the field. However, if the organization's library and patent searching facilities are inadequate, then new developments may not come to the attention of the personnel quickly enough. Moreover, if developments in peripheral fields are not carefully monitored, emerging threats from related technologies may also be missed (see Chapter 2, Section 2.1).

8.3.2. User Needs and Wants

In the case of industrial products, changes in user needs and/or wants can be easily known if the personnel maintain close contact and open interrelationships with the users. Frequent visits to customer facilities by the technical and professional personnel are important, in addition to visits by the marketing personnel. Marketing and technical personnel will observe different details and carry away somewhat different impressions that will add up to an important overall picture. Good communications and respectful, collaborative relationships between the technical and marketing personnel are thus essential in monitoring user needs and wants [3, 4, 5, 6].

In the case of consumer products, continuous market research and surveys of consumer tastes and habits are mandatory. In some product areas (e.g., clothing, beauty and cosmetic items, recreational products, automobiles) consumer tastes can change quite rapidly.

8.3.3. Market Changes and Shifts

Market changes include changes in the price the customer is willing to pay, changes in the total number of customers, changes in the composition of the market (e.g., fewer younger customers and more older customers), changes in the location of the customers, and changes in the way the product is distributed to the customer. For instance, when the U.S. population shifted to the suburbs during the 1940s and 1950s, many shifts occurred in the markets for clothing. Large discount stores opened near the suburban population centers, impersonal selling techniques were emphasized and mass distribution techniques emerged. The price of many types of mass-produced clothing fell, and home-sewn or "hand-made" clothing became relatively extinct.

Thus, market factors are often interrelated and a cascading chain of major changes can occur as a result of a single event. Good market research and an awareness of evolving trends and events are keys to becoming aware of these changes.

8.3.4. Competition

Today, competitive analyses and competitive intelligence collection are important to most businesses. An awareness of what one's competitors are likely to do and what new competitors are likely to emerge is essential to successful project selection and project management. Competitive intelligence gathering has become a legitimate and serious function for most companies. Many firms are developing strategic competitive intelligence systems (SCISs) that integrate their competitive information gathering with their strategic planning functions [7, 8].

8.3.5. Socio-Legal Changes

Environmental regulations, product safety laws, business practices and societal norms have recently become major causes of technical and economic change. Some companies have set up separate departments to watch for changes in environmental regulations and various laws. However, difficulties in communicating emerging changes and observations to project level personnel have sometimes occurred. If top level organizational watchers are used, some mechanism must be provided to link them with project-level personnel.

It is important for project-level personnel to conduct their own informal watching and listening, by reading widely and staying abreast of current affairs. Not only does this provide another perspective, but it broadens and matures the project-level personnel, thereby increasing their general awareness and abilities.

8.4. REPLANNING AND TERMINATION

8.4.1. Replanning and Readjustments

Changes in the cost-progress of a selected project or changes in its environment may cause management to readjust previous selection decisions. Depending on the nature of the changes, several project selection actions are possible, as listed in Table 8.3.

Portfolio readjustments may be made by reallocating funds from one project to another, transferring personnel from one project to another, speeding up the efforts on one project while slowing another, etc. If the changes are severe, the project efforts may be temporarily suspended or backlogged (see Chapter 5, Section 5.0 and 5.1). Or the project may be terminated, and all work on it stopped. In this case, a replacement project may be selected and work begun on the replacement. The replacement project may be selected from the existing backlog or it may be a new entry (see Chapter 5, Section 5.0 and 5.1).

Table 8.3. Some Project Selection Readjustment Actions.

Replanning the project
Readjusting the portfolio of projects
Reallocating funds
Rescheduling the project
Backlogging the project
Reprioritizing the projects
Terminating the project
Replacement with a backlogged project
Replacement with a new project

8.4.2. Terminating Unsuccessful Projects

Some environmental changes, i.e., the disappearance of a market, may make it obvious that a project should be terminated. However, many uncertainties often surround the termination decision. Terminating a project for lack of technical success is usually especially difficult. There are seldom any unequivocal indicators that the project is destined to fail, and should therefore be terminated. The project champions will always be convinced that success is just around the corner, perhaps only a lucky break or the next experiment away. Project terminations are likely to be emotionally traumatic and at least temporarily demotivating for the involved personnel. The way in which the termination occurs can influence the organization's climate for creativity and idea generation for some time into the future [9, 10, 11].

Some indicators that termination should be considered are listed in Table 8.4. Note that these are only indicators. A project should not necessarily be terminated when these indicators arise. Rather, the indicators are red flags that should always trigger an evaluation of the project, and a consideration of termination as one of the alternatives. The indicators listed in Table 8.4 have been frequently (but not always) found to precede the eventual failure of project efforts [9, 11, 12].

The evidence indicates that termination decisions must be made swiftly and replacement projects must be quickly selected [10, 11, 12]. Decisiveness is a key to avoiding morale problems and high opportunity costs in terminations. When a conviction that a project will not succeed sets in and personnel have lost faith in the project, morale problems will already exist. Delaying a termination decision may

Table 8.4. Some Indicators that a Project Should Be Considered for Termination.

Loss of market for the project
Major changes in the market for the product
Loss of faith and enthusiasm by the project personnel
Major changes in the technological difficulty of the project
Major decrease in the likelihood of success of the project
The appearance of potentially insurmountable technological hurdles
Loss of interest in the project by marketing personnel
Loss of interest in the project by top management

needlessly use up resources that could be more productively employed on other projects, thus further exacerbating morale problems. Nothing debilitates an organization quicker than to permit the situation to degenerate into warring factions and endless debates over whether or not a project should be terminated.

A backlog of valuable projects, a constant flow of good ideas and an effective project selection system is an invaluable aid to project terminations. The press of other good alternatives provides a motivation to abandon an effort which has become relatively less attractive. Personnel are always more willing to give up an old idea or project when more attractive alternatives are readily available. Thus, an effective project appraisal and selection system is an invaluable part of the whole project management system.

8.4.3. Transferring Successful Projects

Delays in writing up final reports and passing results on to successor groups like marketing or production can create the same morale problems as delays in making termination decisions. Project personnel need to move swiftly and expeditiously on to the next project assignment.

An often successful approach to transfers is to select the subsequent new project at the point where the completion of the old project is imminent. If work is initiated on the new project in parallel with the finishing up of the old one, work continuity will be promoted. During this transitionary phase, the personnel will work on both projects, or consult for the receiving department (the department that is receiving the project—marketing, production, etc.) while working on the new project. This generally expedites the completion of the old project, and eliminates any uncertainties about work assignments in the minds of the personnel.

To use the above model, a backlog of appraised project ideas must be available for selection. Thus, the appraisal and selection process becomes an essential part of the project termination/transfer management system.

8.5. HANDLING SPINOFFS AND FALLOUTS

Both terminated and completed projects can have a variety of spinoffs and fallouts. New technologies, new know-hows, and other results may be developed that do not have immediate value to the project, but may have future value to the organization. These spinoffs and fallouts may enhance the value of other backlogged projects or new ideas that may be forthcoming. Radical new ideas and valuable projects can rise from the ashes of a failed effort. The sale or license of spinoffs and fallout technologies should always be considered.

In general, spinoffs and fallouts will usually affect the project selection process. The spinoffs and fallouts may result in new ideas and proposals, which will compete with the existing ideas and candidate proposals. Appraising these spinoffs and fallouts may create some problems. Their history of association with successful or terminated efforts may bias some opinions. Assessing them on their own merits and costs—as opposed to assessing them on their joint merits and costs in combination with their parent projects and technologies—may create some analytical obstacles. The reader is referred to Chapter 4, Sections 4.2 through 4.5 and to References 2 and 13 for some solutions to these problems.

8.6. SUMMARY AND CONCLUSIONS

Project appraisal and selection decisions do not end with the selection of a portfolio and the initiation of work on the selected projects. Changes in the status of the projects, cost-progress variances, and unexpected environmental changes can necessitate reappraisal and reselection decisions. Two types of project status changes are commonly encountered: completion and termination. This chapter has discussed some approaches to monitoring selected projects, managing project terminations, handling project completions, and replanning projects in response to unexpected status changes. The need to include project replanning, completion, and termination activities as part of the overall project appraisal/selection system has been repeatedly emphasized.

8.7. REFERENCES

1. Souder, W. E. "Experiences with an R&D Project Control Model," *IEEE Transactions on Engineering Management*, Vol. EM-15, March 1968, pp. 39–49.
2. Souder, W. E. *Management Decision Methods for Managers of Engineering and Research.* New York: Van Nostrand Reinhold, 1980, pp. 308–313.
3. Souder, W. E. "Promoting An Effective R&D/Marketing Interface," *Research Management*, Vol. 23, No. 4, July 1980, pp. 10–15.

4. Souder, W. E. "Disharmony Between R&D and Marketing," *Industrial Marketing Management*, Vol. 10, No. 1, Jan-Feb, 1981, pp. 67–73.
5. Souder, W. E. "Effectiveness of Product Development Methods," *Industrial Marketing Management*. Vol. 7, No. 5, October 1978, pp. 299–307.
6. Souder, W. E. and A. K. Chakrabarti, "The R&D/Marketing Interface: Results from an Empirical Study of Innovation Projects," *IEEE Transactions on Engineering Management*, Vol. EM-25, No. 4, October 1978, pp. 88–93.
7. Souder, E. I. "Design Components for Strategic Competitive Intelligence Systems," *Proceedings of the American Society for Information Science*, Mid-Year Meeting. Durango, Colorado, May 14–16, pp. 157–178, 1981.
8. Souder, W. E. and E. I. Souder. "Strategic Competitive Information Systems (SCIS): Getting to Know Your Competitor Better," to appear.
9. Balachandra, R. and J. A. Raelin. "How To Decide When to Abandon A Project," *Research Management*, Vol. XXII, No. 4, July 1980, pp. 24–29.
10. Fraenkel, S. J. "How Not to Succeed as An R&D Manager," *Research Management*, Vol. XXIII, No. 3, May 1980, pp. 35–37.
11. Holzmann, R. T. "To Stop Or Not: The Big Decision," *Chemtech*, Vol. 2, No. 1, February 1972, pp. 81–89.
12. Souder, W. E. "The Validity of Subjective Probability of Success Forecasts by R&D Managers," *IEEE Transactions on Engineering Management*, Vol. EM-16, No. 1, February 1969, pp. 35–49.
13. Miles, L. D. *Techniques of Value Analysis and Engineering*. New York: McGraw-Hill, 1972.

9. Summary: Managing the System

9.0. SELECTING THE BEST PROJECTS

Engineering, research, and development (ER&D) projects have become increasingly more complex and costly in the past few years. Today's projects often carry large financial and organizational commitments. Incorrect decisions about ER&D ideas and projects can result in technical or commercial failures, and fruitless costs that must be absorbed by the organization. Some ER&D projects are so expensive that these costs may exhaust the organization's resources and severely disrupt its future. Moreover, when an ER&D effort fails, the organization may be doubly penalized: while committed to the unsuccessful project, better opportunities may pass it by [4].

Engineering, research and development projects are often high leverage investments: small dollar decisions made at the ER&D stage can have dramatic impacts and consequences at later points in time. Decisions made on ER&D projects can lock in an organization to designs and technologies for many future years. Judicious ER&D decisions can lead to technological, market, and profit superiority. But poor choices can commit the organization to technologies that are ultimately unsuited to its capabilities. The choice of an inferior project can severely disadvantage the organization in a competitive marketplace, where there is an ever-present danger that a competitor will come up with a better project that captures the entire market.

Thus, it is very important to select only the best projects, and to eliminate inferior projects from consideration before resources are committed to them. However, this is seldom an easy task, since the information and criteria needed to make unequivocal choices is seldom readily available. The properties that distinguish a superior

149

idea from an inferior idea may not be obvious, especially where the ideas relate to an emerging new technology or an embryonic new development. Much of the information used to evaluate candidate ideas and projects will necessarily be judgmental in nature. Thus, individual differences in perspectives, viewpoints, and experiences may influence the appraisals and analyses. Organizational politics, departmental goals, and group loyalties may further influence the decision criteria and procedures.

9.1. COMPONENTS OF A PROJECT SELECTION SYSTEM

This book has presented the state-of-the-art methods for overcoming difficulties in selecting the best projects. Methods were presented which may be applied at the following five stages or components of a project selection and appraisal system: (1) the idea generation and flow component, (2) the information collection component, (3) the analysis and appraisal component, (4) the project selection decision making component, and (5) the project control and reselection component.

In any organization, the choice of ideas and projects will necessarily be delimited by the number and quality of the proposals that are generated. Chapters 2 and 3 discussed the importance of the idea generation and flow component within a project selection system, and presented several useful approaches for stimulating and managing ideas.

Project selection decision making is dependent on the availability of valid and reliable information about the candidate ideas and projects. Thus, it is important to establish systematic procedures and techniques for gathering the needed information, and for properly organizing this information in preparation for project selection decision making. Chapter 4 discussed the state of art methods for this component.

The methods used to reduce, analyze and appraise information are important to any project selection process. Thus, this decision support component [3] should be distinguished from the actual project selection decision making. Chapter 4 presented and discussed the state of the art in this component.

The ability of the organization to recognize and distinguish good proposals from bad proposals is a key factor. This ability will depend in part on the quality of the criteria and decision processes used to judge candidate ideas or proposals. Different criteria and decision processes will be appropriate, depending on the nature of the proposals, the available information, the goals of the organization and the decision setting environment [2]. It is essential that appropriate criteria and decision processes be applied, in a consistent and systematic fashion, as rigorously as possible. Chapters 5, 6, and 7 presented methods for developing and using high quality criteria and effective decision process aids.

The project selection and appraisal process does not end with the selection of a project and the start of work on it. Events may occur during the life of the project that will make it relatively more or less attractive than other alternatives. As discussed in Chapter 8, these events may be internal to the project (e.g., poor cost and schedule performance) or they may be external to the project (e.g., the sudden appearance of a competing technology). Thus, a reselection of projects may occur. Management may decide to reallocate funds to speed up or slow down the efforts, the project work may be replanned and modified, or the project may be terminated and replaced by a new one. The successful completion of a project creates a reselection situation because it frees resources that can be devoted to another project. Thus, project selection is a recurrent process. Chapter 8 presented and discussed the state-of-the-art methods for carrying out this control and reselection process.

9.2. DESIGNING AND MANAGING THE PROJECT SELECTION SYSTEM

As this book has shown, project selection and evaluation should be viewed as a *total system* of component activities, ranging from idea generation to project termination. It is important to use the best state-of-the-art techniques in performing each of these component activities. However, it is essential to appreciate the interconnections between these components, and to view them as a total system. The overemphasis of one component at the neglect of another will lead to a lopsided system, with ineffective selection decisions and disappointing projects [1, 2, 4].

Designing and managing project selection systems is a primary responsibility of technical management—the managers of engineering, research and development. Such systems can be especially valuable for focusing attention on key issues, stimulating open communication and interaction, and establishing a sound basis for subsequent project management. However, a purely mechanical approach to the design and use of project selection systems is not effective. Systems are energized and activated by people [2, 5]. The successful project selection systems designer must understand methods *and* human behavior. An effective system combines human talents and decision aids in order to integrate human judgments and analytical processes [1, 2]. Successful technical managers are masters of the art of combining project selection methods, technical knowledge, and interpersonal skills. They use this combined art to help them identify valuable ideas, rally enthusiastic organizational support for them, and promote successful projects from these ideas. Thus, in addition to acquiring a working knowledge of the methods in this book, the successful technical manager must be proficient in communications, interpersonal behavior, and social skills. (See Appendexes A and B.)

Designing and managing an effective project selection system is a major challange for most of today's organizations. Tomorrow's leaders will come from the ranks of those who are able to meet today's challenge.

9.3. REFERENCES

1. Souder, W. E. *Management Decision Methods for Managers of Engineering and Research.* New York: Van Nostrand Reinhold, 1980, pp. 137–162.
2. Souder, W. E. *Management Decision Methods for Managers of Engineering and Research.* New York: Van Nostrand Reinhold, 1980, pp. 301–313.
3. Vazonyi, Andre, "Decision Support Systems: The New Technology of Decision Making," Interfaces, Vol. 9, No. 1, 1978, pp. 72–77.
4. Souder, W. E. "Disharmony Between R&D and Marketing," *Industrial Marketing Management*, Vol. 10, No. 1, Jan–Feb 1981, pp. 67–73.
5. Gibson, J. L., J. M. Ivancevich, and J. H. Donnelly. *Organizations.* Dallas: Irwin-Dorsey, 1982.

Appendix A. Management Decision Methods[1]

What really is a "decision"? Is it an event? An occurrence? A behavioral process? A mental process? These are surprisingly difficult questions to answer. A decision would seem to be all of these and more. Yet a precise definition is very elusive.

A decision is a very personal thing that occurs internal to the individual. Judgment and intuition are involved, as are sentiments and individual value systems. We never really get to see a decision. We only see its manifestations and effects. We can observe how individuals and groups go about making a decision. We can document their behavior patterns and the analytical methods used. We can describe the sequence of logic used, the factors influencing the decision and the rationale for the final choices that are made. But it can hardly be said that we have observed a decision. Rather, we have observed only the elements of a decision process. These elements consist of the behavior patterns, the analytical procedures and the sequence of logic used in making a decision. Thus, while a decision may be a mysterious thing, the elements of a decision making process are not. They are visible, tangible and controllable. And they can be structured in such a way that they comprise a highly objective and systematic approach to decision making.

A.1. ELEMENTS OF DECISION MAKING

A.1.1. Model of a Decision Process

Though decision processes usually differ with the nature of the problem, the situation and the individual decision maker, Figure A.1 presents a general picture of most decision processes. This model depicts decisions as being precipitated by the recognition of problems or opportunities. If the

---

[1] This appendix is based on Wm. E. Souder, *Management Decision Methods for Managers of Engineering and Research*, Van Nostrand Reinhold, 1980, pp. 3–26.

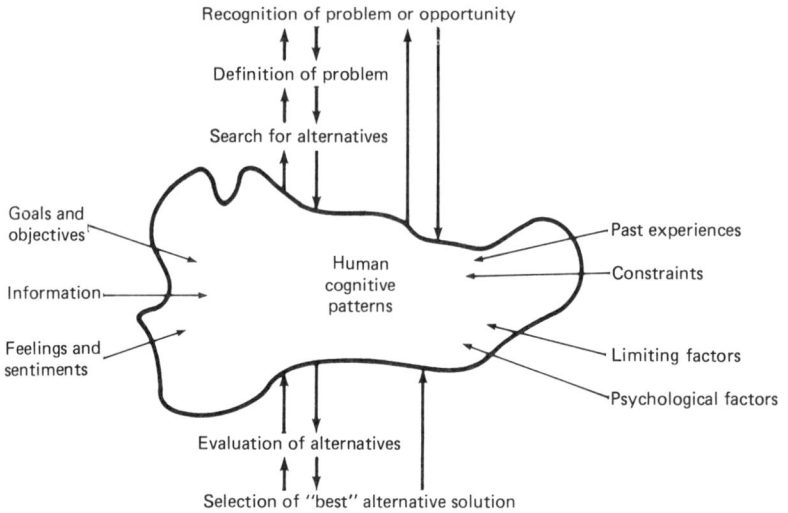

Figure A.1. Elements of a decision making process.

problem or opportunity is perceived as a routine one, the decision maker may go immediately to the selection of the best alternative solution. If the problem or opportunity is a familiar one, then little time may be devoted to its definition. If the problem or opportunity is well-defined, then the search for alternative solutions or ways to take advantage of the opportunity may be brief. If the relative effectiveness of the alternatives are known, then very little time may be spent in analyzing and evaluating the alternatives and deliberating about the best one.

In terms of Figure A.1, the nature of the problem may influence whether or not the decision maker moves through the process slowly or quickly. If the problem is a routine one that is solved by habit, then the decision maker may jump from problem recognition to the selection of the best alternative solution. If the decision is one that has been preprogrammed, then the decision maker may skip the problem definition and the search for alternatives. In a preprogrammed decision there are a finite number of alternatives with known effectiveness, and the decision maker must match up the appropriate alternative with the problem stimulus. An example is deciding what clothes to wear in the morning. The problem stimuli include the weather and the planned daily activities. Sunny, warm weather and recreational activities require one kind of wardrobe, while other weather and other activities require different appropriate dress.

If the decision problem is complex or poorly understood then the decision process may be quite lengthy and deliberative. As Figure A.1 shows, there may be considerable recycling back and forth within the process. The search for alternatives may result in information that further clarifies the problem or suggests its redefinition. New alternatives may be discovered during the processes of evaluating and analyzing the original set of alternatives. The best alternative may not be apparent from the original set, and a new search for alternatives may be undertaken. Thus, the decision making process may be very heuristic and iterative in nature.

A.1.2. The Human Aspects

The model in Figure A.1 depicts human cognitive patterns as being at the center of the overall decision making process. These patterns are largely unknown and unobservable to us. We know that personal values, goals and organizational objectives can strongly influence the decision maker. In part, these influences explain why two individuals may not perceive a problem in the same way, or may not select the same final solution. Goals and objectives, the level of available information, the individual's feelings, the individual's psychological makeup, and a host of other variables may deeply influence the perception of the problem, the evaluation of the alternatives, and other elements of the decision making process.

Unfortunately, we can't easily look inside human thought processes to see precisely how these patterns operate. Thus, attempts to directly improve actual human thought patterns are stymied. But, as Figure A.1 shows, a substantial number of important elements in the overall decision making process are not locked up within the human cognitive area. These elements can be made more rational, systematic and complete through the direct application of improved methods and techniques. By improving these elements, human thought processes may then be indirectly impacted and improved.

A.2. THE STRUCTURED DECISION MAKING PROCESS

Figure A.2 presents an algorithm for the structured decision making process. This algorithm describes the various steps that are performed within the structured decision making process, and shows the relationships between them. The algorithm builds on the model presented in Figure A.1.

This algorithm is a general one that applies to a variety of types of problems and situations. Let us examine each of the various steps within the algorithm and the procedures for carrying them out.

A.2.1. Recognizing a Problem or Opportunity

The first indication of the existence of a problem or an opportunity comes as a variance between the actual conditions and the established standards, or the desired conditions. If there are no standards, or if the standards are poorly established, then there is a good chance that the problem or opportunity may go unrecognized much longer than it should have. This capability to have early warnings of pending problems or opportunities is perhaps one of the most convincing arguments for engaging in thorough planning and standard-setting. Early detection often makes the difference between success and failure in decision making. But if there are no plans or comparative standards, then one has no way of determining whether a problem or opportunity exists.

Problem and opportunity recognition is a highly personal and subjective process. It may be influenced by a variety of personal filters and barriers. Habits, past experiences, aspirations, and many other personal behavioral variables can influence whether or not a situation becomes a part of an individual's cognitive awareness. These factors also influence whether or not the individual admits the situation into the cognitive list of important problems or opportunities. Thus, problem and opportunity recognition is a two-step personal process of seeing and admitting. I may see a problem, but I may not think it is important or significant. If I don't think its important, it won't motivate me to action. The result will be the same as if I had not seen the problem at all.

Many problems and opportunities are not recognized in a timely fashion because the decision maker cannot discriminate between relevant and irrelevant information. Situations typically contain a great deal of information that is irrelevant to the real problem. To be effective, a decision maker must develop the skills to sort out important from unimportant information. The decision maker must also be alert and sensitive to the market, technological, economic, legal, and political environments that surround the problem or opportunity. The market, economic, and technological environments will determine whether or not the problem or opportunity is one that can wait or must be acted upon now. The legal and political environments will determine whether the event is a problem or an opportunity. For instance, antipollution laws are problems for some heavy industries, but they provide many opportunities for pollution control firms. Enterprising and alert organizations can often find creative ways to turn problems into opportunities if they can gain sufficient lead time by examining the emerging technical, social, and political trends.

The setting in which the problem arises will often greatly influence its perception. An individual may perceive a problem that is not recognized by others. In an individual decision setting, action may be taken immediately. But in a group or organizational setting, this same problem might not be acted upon at all unless all the parties recognize it.

Thus, there are many individual, situational and environmental filters that can cloud the problem or opportunity recognition process. The alert decision maker will examine all variances between the actual conditions and the standard by asking the following four questions:

1. Is this a variance that could have major technical, social, legal, economic, or political ramifications?
2. Could these ramifications produce either problems or opportunities for the organization, the decision maker, or other concerned parties?
3. Is the variance greater than the random variations that could normally be expected?
4. Is the variance likely to increase if no action is taken now?

If the answer to any of these four questions is "yes", then the decision maker cannot afford to ignore the variance. An in-depth analysis of the nature of the variance and its implications is warranted.

A.2.2. Problem and Opportunity Definition

Problems and opportunities almost never present themselves in a well-defined fashion. The first visible tip of the iceberg is the symptoms. But operating on symptoms will normally be ineffective. The decision maker must peel through the onionlike layers of symptoms until the real issues are confronted.

This is no easy matter. The available information will be a mixture of random facts, feelings, complaints, prejudices, inferences and opinions about the situation. During the early stages, it will be difficult to distinguish relevant from irrelevant information. But, as more information is acquired, this distinction will gradually emerge. The process of probing for more information and the sorting of fact from fancy will take time and require perseverence. The organizational climate must encourage and support these efforts, which will compete for the manager's limited time and energies. The entire process of problem and opportunity definition is often a very discontinuous, groping action. It requires a patience and belief in the potential pay-off. But anyone who has attempted to treat symptoms knows from first-hand experience how important it is to get to the real problem.

The price for operating on symptoms can be a missed opportunity or an unsolved problem, on top of the wasted time and resources spent on ineffective treatments. It is nearly always cheaper in the long run to search out the real, underlying problems and opportunities. Few decisions fail because the wrong alternatives are chosen. But many decisions fail because the wrong problem was solved. An adequate investment in problem definition efforts is perhaps the highest payoff investment that can be made in the whole decision making process.

To assist the decision maker in defining the problem or opportunity, some characterization and identification procedures are available. However, these are only aids or guidelines. Their application requires a great deal of incisive inquiry and dogged detective work. Let us briefly look at these procedures.

(a) Problem and Opportunity Characterization. Every variance should be characterized by its time and location of occurrence. Such when-and-where diagnoses help to distinguish what the problem *is* from what it *is not.* The decision maker should always ask, "What is it *not?*" This helps to narrow down the list of possible problems or opportunities. The determination of the time and location of the variance tells us where to look for additional diagnostic information, and serves as a guideline in distinguishing relevant from irrelevant information. For example, suppose we can state that an observed difference between the actual and desired product performance has the following time and location characteristics: It seems to originate in the quality control department, it occurs only during the third production shift, and it never occurs on Tuesdays. These statements help to direct and focus the search for additional relevant information that will define and clarify the real problem or opportunity.

(b) Problem And Opportunity Identification. This approach identifies the specific nature and properties of the variance. A written identification statement is developed that specifies:

1. The specific standard that has been violated;
2. The implications of this;
3. The potential and actual problems or opportunities which this creates;
4. The most serious, urgent, immediate or otherwise prominent problem or opportunity from the list of potential ones;
5. Whose opportunity or problem it is, in terms of responsibilities, and under what circumstances.

When these identification and characterization procedures are combined, they provide a comprehensive approach to the definition of the specific problem or opportunity. This definition includes an information base for further decision making, it identifies the person responsible for taking further actions, and it provides some direction for this action.

A.2.3. Enumeration of Alternatives

The process of generating alternatives is seldom given the attention it deserves. Many decision makers spend a great deal of effort on the evaluation and selection of alternatives, and very little time generating alternatives. Because the quality of a decision can be no better than the quality of the alternatives that are available, it is important to devote an adequate amount of time to the generation of high-quality alternatives.

The development of alternative solutions is often a very heuristic process. It is also a very delicate creative process. Thus, the application of various creativity and idea generating methods are often needed at this stage of the process. Experience shows that behavioral process controls and group management methods are also important, since ideas are more easily produced in a nonevaluative atmosphere. Combinations of alternatives should be sought, both as a springboard for generating more creative ideas and as viable combined solutions. Combined solutions are often needed when the problem is highly complex.

The do-nothing alternative is always an admissible policy. It should always appear in the list of possible alternative decisions. It may not turn out to be a viable alternative. But it should always be as painstakingly analyzed as any other potential action. The alternative of doing nothing is sometimes written off all too quickly, and the decision maker rushes into commitments that turn out to be much worse choices. The exercise of considering and analyzing the do-nothing alternative can lead to an enlightened picture of the decision problem, which may trigger the generation of other creative alternatives.

It should be noted that deciding to do nothing and procrastinating are two very different things. A decision maker who *decides* to do nothing has gone through a logical decision process. But a decision maker who has not gone through a decision process does not really know whether the do-nothing alternative is the best or the worst. Procrastination suggests that the decision maker is unskilled, indecisive, and ineffective in decision making.

A.2.4. Specifying Goals

The goals which the decision maker wishes to achieve by solving the problem must be clearly stated at the outset. The goals represent the desired state of affairs. They serve as the basis for measuring the effectiveness of the alternatives. And they serve as indicators that tell us when the problem is solved. Quite simply, the problem is not completely solved until all the goals are achieved. If the best available alternatives cannot be expected to achieve all the goals, then more effective alternatives should be sought before the decision maker commits to a final decision.

The goals and the standards (see Figure A.2) must articulate closely with each other. The standards are the specific, detailed benchmarks which translate the goals into measurable targets. The standard is the statement of the acceptable level of achievement of the goal. For example, if the goal is to maximize sales volume, then the corresponding standard should specify the level of sales volume targeted during some time horizon. If the standards

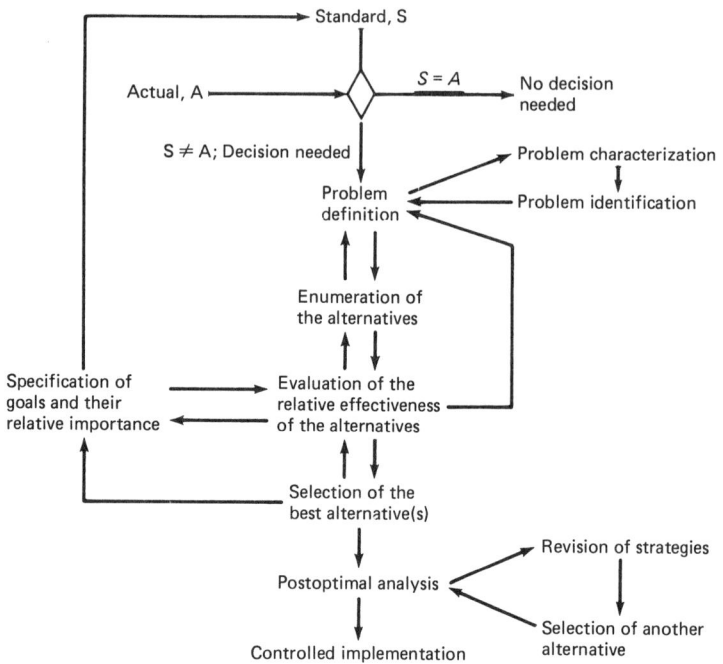

Figure A.2. Algorithm for the structured decision making process.

are set too high this may lead to underachievements and to false signals of problems or opportunities when there are none. The failure to achieve a high standard may demotivate future achievements, and cause the standards to be set too low in the next planning cycle. This may result in the adoption of less ambitious goals. If the standards are set too low then the system will never sense any problems or opportunities, even though they may abound.

Real goals are not always apparent, and hard thought is sometimes needed to develop a precise statement of the desired state of affairs. This is often the case in group and organizational settings, where the various individuals and departments may collectively have many dissimilar and conflicting goals. Even an individual decision maker may have multiple goals and several desired levels of achievements. A good starting point in ascertaining goals and standards is to simply ask the following two questions: "What is the desired state of affairs?" and "How would you know when the problem is solved?" This usually evokes a set of criteria which embody the goals and standards. For example, suppose the decision maker responds that the problem would be solved when sales return to the desired three billion dollar per year level. In this case, the three billion dollar level is both a goal and a standard.

A.2.5. Evaluating Alternatives

Each alternative must be analyzed and evaluated in terms of its value, cost and risk characteristics. The value of an alternative is measured in terms of its contributions to the achievement of each of the goals. The value of each alternative should be assessed in terms of the benefits that can be expected to result if it is chosen, and in terms of the regrets that can be suffered if it is *not chosen*. A focus on the regrets that may occur by not choosing a particular alternative can often be very revealing. In some cases, the regrets for an alternative may be so enormous that it must be chosen in order to protect the organization's current position.

The cost of each alternative must be carefully assessed in terms of its out-of-pocket costs, opportunity costs, and follow-on costs. The out-of-pocket costs are the day-to-day expenses and capital outlays which the organization must pay out to finance the alternative. Opportunity costs are hidden costs, e.g., the interest foregone on invested capital or other opportunities foregone because funds are invested in this alternative. The follow-on costs of each alternative should be very carefully examined. It is not unusual to find that an alternative which looks inexpensive may require massive capital at some later date to implement or maintain it.

The risk characteristics of each alternative should be carefully assessed, in terms of the likelihoods of achieving each of the goals. Some high-valued alternatives may have the potential to make very large contributions to the achievement of the goals. However, the likelihood that they will actually accomplish these potentials may be very small. Other, medium-valued alternatives may exhibit a high degree of certainty of making moderate contributions. Thus, when their risk characteristics are taken into account, the medium-valued alternatives may be the higher-contributing choices.

In most decision situations, multiple goals will exist. Some of the goals will be more important than others. These differences in importance need to be carefully expressed as a basis for distinguishing between the alternatives. An alternative that contributes to a highly important goal will generally be a higher-valued alternative than one that contributes to a less important goal.

A.2.6. Selecting the Best Alternative

Theoretically, the alternatives can be ranked from best to worst on the basis of some benefit/cost, regret/cost, or risk/cost ratios. However, it is not possible to include all the relevant factors in such an index. Some of these relevant factors are: the efficiency with which the alternative solves the problem, the impact of the alternative on the various noneconomic organizational goals, the acceptability of the alternative to those who will implement and use it, the changes in behavior patterns required if the alternative is chosen, and the interrelationships between the alternatives. In group or organizational settings, there may be many different persons who are involved in the final decision. These persons may be suppliers of decision information, decision makers, or decision influencers. Thus, the selection process may be influenced by many behavioral factors.

Judgment, bargaining, and analytical processes may often be used in selecting the best alternative. In the judgmental approach, an individual makes an intuitive choice from among the alternatives. The judgmental approach is often so intuitive that it is not easily documented or explained to another decision maker. Bargaining is a process by which a group of decision makers with conflicting goals exercise judgments, converse about them, and then trade off wants and desires until some agreement is reached. The analytical approach involves factual evaluations and rigorous comparisons of the alternatives on the basis of costs, benefits, regrets, and other measures. The analytical approach includes a quantitiative and procedural measurement of values and costs. Political activities may also occur. They generally manifest themselves in the use of bargaining routines by those who have some control over the choices. In organizational settings, the final decision may have to be approved by many different layers in the organization. Thus, there may be many opportunities for bargaining and political activities in an organizational decision making setting.

In the structured decision process, the best alternative is selected on the basis of the application of analytical models and techniques. Operations research and management science methods are used to help the decision maker select the optimum choice, on the basis of economic considerations. Political activities are thus kept to a minimum by focusing on objective processes and rigorous analyses. However, systematic and controlled judgments are incorporated into the process at various points, in order to include noneconomic and nonquantifiable considerations. Controlled bargaining may also be necessary at some points, in order to arrive at a decision that balances off all the various needs and desires. Sometimes a single best alternative may be chosen. Sometimes several alternatives may be found to be satisfactory. More often, no one alternative will be the best on all the criteria or under all the considerations. Then, a package of alternatives may be devised. Or several alternatives may be selected for implementation in a sequence of steps, ranging from the least risky to the most risky.

A.2.7. Postoptimal Analysis

The best or optimum decision for the conditions confronting the decision maker may not be the best choice under some other conditions. Using management science models and methods, a postoptimal analysis can be made to check the sensitivity of the optimum decision to changes in the decision conditions. If the optimum decision is not found to be the best decision over the entire range of possible conditions, then several strategies are available. The postoptimal analysis may be used to find combinations of alternatives that are effective over the entire range of conditions. Contingency plans may be developed. Or a multi-echelon decision approach may be taken, where various alternatives are implemented as the emerging conditions warrant.

The postoptimal analysis also provides an opportunity for the decision maker to review all the preceding steps in the structured decision making process. The logic chain and sequence of activities can be checked. And any new information or alternatives that may have arisen during the process can be taken into account at this time.

A.2.8. Controlled Implementation

A decision is absolutely worthless if it cannot be implemented. Anyone who takes the time and effort to make a decision that cannot be implemented may be worse off than if no decision had been made. Once the time, effort and funds have been expended the decision maker may develop an emotional attachment to the decision. It may then be difficult to convince the decision maker that this particular decision is impractical or unacceptable to those who must use it.

A decision is not complete until a plan for its implementation has been devised. The development of an effective implementation plan is every bit as important as the decision itself. This plan should specify the barriers and obstacles to the acceptance of the decision, and the ways in which these are to be overcome through motivational and behavioral changes. Because of the nature of people in general, abrupt changes in human behavior should not be expected. Thus, the implementation should be spread over a reasonable time span. In general, the most difficult decisions to implement are those which involve major changes in human behaviors, those which have uncertain effects and far-reaching implications, those which involve personal risks to the individual decision makers, or those which involve large commitments of resources. These are precisely the characteristics of most managerial decisions.

Implementation will be facilitated where the following three things are done. First, implementation should be considered during the evaluation and analysis of the alternatives. Any alternative that is not implementable should not be considered further. Any alternatives that are difficult to implement should be considered only as a last resort. Second, the implementation of any alternative will be improved where those who have to use it are participatively involved in its formulation. Not only will the users be more willing to accept something they have had a hand in, but the actual quality of the decision may also be improved. Finally, attention must be given to selling the alternative. Those who must accept and use the new decision must understand how it can help them, and they must be enthusiastic about it. The decision maker must always keep in mind the motives of those who are expected to adopt and use the decision.

A.3. SOME ROADBLOCKS

There are several human traits and proclivities that can diminish the effectiveness of the structured decision making process unless they are carefully guarded against. By being aware of these roadblocks, the decision maker will be in a better position to avoid them.

A.3.1. Jumping from Problem to Solution

It is human nature to jump from problem to solution, and to circumvent an explicit algorithmic process. We all have a proclivity to rely on our innate abilities. There is a tendency to feel that reliance on any decision models or algorithmic aids somehow diminishes our own personal abilities. But intuitive processes do not give any assurances that some information or some alternative has not been missed. To be sure that "all the bases have been touched", an explicit algorithm like the structured decision process must be followed.

A.3.2. Premature Evaluation

When first confronted with a problem, it is human nature to want to immediately search for causes and solutions. But it is usually more important to search for more information about the problem itself. An expanded diagnosis of the what, when, where, how, and why of the problem is necessary before an enlightened search for causes and solutions can occur. Otherwise there is a very great danger of solving the wrong problem.

A.3.3. Over-Reliance on Experience

Most of us have experienced the déjà-vu phenomenon of having "been here before." As our experiences grow and we become successful in decision making, many elements of the new situations we encounter are indeed much like some we have encountered before. This can be a dangerous trap. It encourages us to apply old solutions that have succeeded in the past. The danger is that all of us suffer from incomplete recall. And the new situation is often just enough different that the old solutions do not apply. Thus, what seems like an old problem may mysterously fail to respond to our tried and proven ways. This is a very great danger for the decision maker who becomes complacent and overconfident as a result of past successes.

A.3.4. Premature Commitment

Finding a satisfactory solution too early in the process can blind the decision maker to better solutions. This is especially the case where the problem appears to be a familiar one. The decision maker may become so emotionally committed to this one satisfactory alternative that others simply do not penetrate this blind commitment. Maintaining an open mind and a healthy skepticism toward older, well-tried solutions is a protection against this roadblock.

A.3.5. Confusion of Problems and Symptoms

There is a natural human tendency to deal with problems at face value. Consequently, many symptoms are mistaken for problems. The decision maker should always maintain that a hidden agenda exists, under the layers of first impressions and awarenesses. It is always more costly in the long run to overlook a problem. Looking for a hidden problem and being disappointed is seldom a great waste of effort or funds, relative to the enormous regrets that can result from failing to look.

A.3.6. Focusing on One Solution

Most real problems are a complex bundle of interrelated smaller problems. Thus, it is unlikely that a single alternative solution will be completely effective. A combination or system of articulated solutions is usually needed This salient fact is often overlooked. Many decision makers seek the unreachable, all-purpose single solution. This is usually unrealistic.

A.3.7. Overlooking Implementation

There is a tendency to gloss over the implementation aspects. The fact that no solution implements itself is often overlooked. Frequently, more time and effort are needed in implementing the solution than it takes to find and develop it. A sensitive and realistic decision maker is aware of the natural human resistances to change, and these considerations are taken into account in the choices and actions.

A.4. TECHNICAL VERSUS MANAGERIAL DECISIONS

A.4.1. Technical Decisions

Traditional engineering and scientific decisions primarily involve the application of established principles of physics, chemistry, mathematics, and other sciences. Engineering and scientific problems are usually well-identified. The decision alternatives are usually fairly well-known. The performance data to evaluate the relative effectiveness of the alternatives are either at hand or obtainable through measurements and laboratory experiments. The data are objective and demonstrable. The optimum decision can be chosen on the basis of established physical laws and rational engineering calculations.

Today, technical decision making is much less straightforward. Society and technology are so interwoven that there is hardly any technical decision that does not have some effect on the quality of life. Today's technical decisions invariably involve some trade-offs between technical, economic and social factors. The choice of the optimum chemical process, the most effective design, or the most marketable product can have many far-reaching legal, social, and economic consequences. These consequences can affect many different parties, sometimes for many years into the future. Modern-day technical decision makers cannot afford to be insensitive to the systems aspects and the human impacts of their decisions. Engineers and scientists must be able to integrate human and nonhuman considerations into their decisions. Modern technical decision making involves a sensitivity to organizations, institutions, people, and society as well as technology.

Thus, modern day engineers and scientists have a substantial need to rely on the structured decision making process, and to avail themselves of its benefits. Without the rigor and systematic procedures which the structured decision process supplies, it would be easy for modern engineers and scientists to lose their way in decision making. They must traverse a maze of decision factors, a variety of multiple goals, and the often conflicting needs of safety, profitability, and technical performance.

A.4.2. Management Decisions

Technical decisions primarily impact on things. Management decisions primarily impact on people. Moreover, management decisions characteristically involve large commitments of resources. Technical decisions are usually much more micro in their orientation. Management decisions are usually clouded by a great deal of uncertainty. Technical decision makers have relatively more information, concepts, theories, and tangible foundations for their choices. Managers often deal with situations where information is almost completely lacking. A manager's decisions are usually risky, and they may have very long-lasting consequences.

Thus, large elements of judgment, intuition, and experience characterize management decisions. Because of this, the manager's individual personality will often deeply influence the decision making style and the decision outcomes. However, an exclusive reliance on managerial personalities is a handicraft approach to decision making. A complete reliance on individual personalities would lead to uncoordinated chaos in organizational decision making. Thus, the further away we get from the well-ordered world of technical decision making and the closer we get to the less-structured world of managerial decision making, the more important it becomes to use the structured decision process. The structured decision process becomes all-important for focusing decision behaviors and controlling haphazardness in management decision behaviors.

A.4.3. A New Era

Today's managers face a whole new era of challenges. Government, labor unions, consumers, stockholders, suppliers, and a host of other groups are all of concern to today's managers. Many different demands are placed on the modern manager in satisfying these groups.

Today's manager must thus play the role of an innovator, a negotiator, a fireman, a motivator, and a resource allocator in the decision making process. The innovator role demands that the manager lead the organization into new products, new fields, and new technologies. As a negotiator, the manager must bargain, compromise, and harmonize various groups and factions. As a fireman, the modern manager must be alert to small disturbances and be decisive in eliminating them. Today's manager must be able to motivate others to action. The successful manager is decisive in allocating resources to competing projects and effective in setting timely priorities.

Thus, today's manager must supplement experience and intuition with more powerful tools and processes. Organized and systematic processes are necessary in order to cope with the demands of this new era. The structured decision process and its associated techniques and methods can be a potent tool, especially when combined with seasoned judgment.

A.5. FROM SCIENTIST/ENGINEER TO MANAGER

A.5.1. Science versus Management

Scientists and engineers are trained and sensitized to use methodical logic and objective thinking. They are trained to make conclusions and solve problems through the application of theorems and proofs. They are taught to seek unequivocal evidence before coming to a final conclusion. The formal training of a scientist or an engineer emphasizes an analytical capability and the scientific approach. The focus is on finding exact solutions to well-defined problems, by the use of objective data and established theories. Sound technical decision making depends on the ability to apply rigorous methods in searching out causes and solutions to problems.

By contrast, managerial decision making requires an ability to size up people and situations, with only a minimum of information about *symptoms.* An effective manager is able to diagnose a situation when only a very small amount of the problem iceberg is visible. This is in direct contrast to the scientific approach. The scientific approach to decision making uses a large volume of well-ordered information, which is sifted and evaluated in the light of established theories and concepts. By contrast, a manager may modify the theory with each new problem. Management theories are often nebulous and tentative, and are often based on a few individual cases. In effect, the manager has relatively few established rules and principles to rely on.

These differences may pose considerable problems for the young scientist or engineer who has just been advanced to a managerial level position. For others, the transition may be less difficult because they have a latent reservoir of managerial talents. This reservoir may be an inherited trait, it may be due to early experiences, or some combination of both. For most scientists and engineers, managerial abilities must be acquired. They can best be acquired through a combination of formal training in a university classroom and on the job experiences. This exposes the individual to a combination of theory and practice that reinforce each other. This combination of formal and experiential training is all the more important in today's complex society, where manager's are confronted with a vast new era of challenges.

A.5.2. The Technical Manager

In today's new era of management challenges, there are ever increasing needs for individuals who understand technology and who can effectively manage human resources in harnessing that technology. Moreover, because we live in a management class oriented culture, many engineers and scientists aspire to managerial positions. Thus, the technical manager has become a very important and prevalent member of today's management ranks.

A technical manager is an individual who manages research, development, engineering, and other technological functions. The job may carry titles like group leader, section leader, project manager, product manager, R&D manager, or vice president of technology. The content of the function may be primarily technical, as in the case of a group leader. Or it may be primarily administrative, as in the case of a vice president of technology. All technical management functions are especially demanding and challenging. They require the individual to be both a capable technical decision maker and a capable manager. The successful technical manager must be able to partition technical and managerial skills, bringing them to bear on different problems at different points of time. The technical manager must recognize which skill is being demanded and when to draw on how much of each. The technical manager must be able to distinguish between a technical problem and a managerial problem, or a problem that is some combination of both. In short, the technical manager must be able to play both the role of the scientist or engineer and the role the manager. A technical manager must have the ability to move between whichever role is demanded at that particular point in time.

Because the methods of science and management differ, the ability to move smoothly between these two roles is not easily acquired. In the technical role, the individual is inclined to seek out salient facts that lead directly to a solution. There is a strong inclination to seek exact conclusions to some salient portion of the overall problem. But most managerial situations require that the decision maker distinguish symptoms from causes and understand the *whole* problem, in its total setting. Satisfactory resolutions of the whole problem are sought by achieving some balance among the human and technical aspects.

When the structured decision process is properly applied, it can help the technical manager distinguish the technical and managerial roles. It can increase the effectiveness of management decision making by integrating some scientific methodologies with some judgmental approaches. The structured decision process is especially well-adapted to assist the technical manager.

A.6. SUMMARY

A decision involves many intuitive and deep-seated cognitive mechanisms that cannot be observed or directly influenced. What can be influenced are the behavior patterns, the analytical procedures, and the sequences of logic that are followed in making a decision. These are the elements of the decision making process.

The elements are often haphazard, unsystematic, inefficient, and ineffective. Improvements may be sought through the application of the structured decision making process. Improvements can be expected in the following eight areas. One, more timely sensing and recognition of emerging problems and opportunities will result. This will enable the decision maker to have more time to devote to the problem and to take earlier actions. Two, a greater depth of comprehension and a more accurate identification of the real problems and opportunities will result. Thus, the chances of operating on false symptoms or solving the wrong problems will be reduced. Three, more logical and higher quality alternative decision choices and strategies will result. Since the quality of the final decision is limited by the quality of the available alternatives, improvements in the alternatives will translate directly into improvements in the final decision. Four, a detailed specification of the articulated goals and standards will be developed. This will tie the problem-solving activities closely to the organizational or individual goals and the long range plans. Five, a comprehensive evaluation of the benefits, costs and regrets of each alternative will be undertaken. The resulting expanded information base will permit the decision maker to exercise more enlightened judgments. Six, intuition, bargaining and political processes will be reduced in favor of more rigorous, systematic comparative analyses as the basis for selecting the overall best alternative. Seven, contingency plans and other preparations will be more effectively developed. Eight, through the use of behavioral techniques and group methods, the chances that the decision will be implemented will be increased.

Today's managers are confronted with decision making challenges of unparalleled complexity. Society and technology have become so interwoven that the successful manager must be able to synergize an entire system of human, political, economic, social, ethical, legal, and technical factors. A large element of judgment is required in solving modern management problems. But reliance on judgment alone is not sufficient to cope with today's demands. A much more structured, more systematic and more powerful decision making process is needed.

A.7. BIBLIOGRAPHY

Badawy, M. K. "Easing the Switch from Engineer to Manager," *Machine Design*, May 15, 1975, pp. 66–68.

Braybrooke, David and C. E. Lindblom. *A Strategy of Decisions*. New York: Free Press, 1963.

Cleland, D. I. and W. R. King. *Management: A Systems Approach*. New York: McGraw-Hill, 1972.

Duncan, W. J. *Decision Making and Social Issues*. Hinsdale, Ill.: Dryden, 1973.

Ebert, R. J. and T. R. Mitchell. *Organizational Decision Processes*. New York: Crane, Russak & Company, 1975.

Estes, R. M. "The Business-Society Relationship: Emerging Major Issues," in *Selected Major Issues in Businesses' Role in Modern Society*, G. A. Steiner (ed.). Los Angeles, California: UCLA Graduate School of Management, 1973.

Hallenberg, E. X. "Dual Advancement Ladder Provides Unique Recognition for the Scientist," *Research Management*, Vol. 13, No. 3, 1970, pp. 221–227.

Handschumacher, A. G. "The Scientist. Is He Equipped for Managing?" *Office Executive*, April 1961, pp. 20–21.

Kimblin, C. W. and W. E. Souder. "Maintaining Staff Productivity as Half-Life Decreases," *Research Management*, Vol. 18, No. 6, 1975, pp. 29–35.

Simon, H. A. *The New Science of Management Decision*. New York: Harper and Row, 1960.

Souder, W. E., *Management Decision Methods for Managers of Engineering and Research*. New York: Van Nostrand Reinhold, 1980.

Sutherland, J. W. *Administrative Decision-Making*. New York: Van Nostrand-Reinhold, 1977.

Tagiuri, Renato. "Value Orientations of Managers and Scientists," in *Administering Research and Development*, C. D. Orth, J. C. Bailey, and F. W. Wolek (eds.). Homewood, Ill.: Irwin, 1964, pp. 63–71.

Appendix B. The Transition from Engineering to Management[1]

Many young engineers will choose lifelong rewarding careers in engineering. Others will choose to move into fulfilling management careers. Still others will become victims of "career drift," moving aimlessly through a variety of unrewarding jobs.

A rewarding and challenging lifelong career is central to the well-being, happiness, and development of every individual. How can a young engineer achieve this desired state of affairs? How can career drift be avoided? What factors should be considered in choosing between staying in engineering or moving into management? Career planning can answer these questions.

B.1. CAREER PLANNING

Career planning is the continuous process through which an individual plans for professional growth, the orderly progression of future jobs, and the assumption of increased responsibilities. A career plan is the roadmap that results from this planning process. The roadmap specifies the best ways for an individual to grow and develop, through a related succession of job milestones.

Career planning can help to insure that assignments are consistent with the engineer's life goals. It can help engineers decide whether to stay primarily in technical work or move to administrative work, and how and when to make this transition. For those engineers who decide to remain in technical work, career planning can help to insure that their assignments are challenging and rewarding, and that they do not become technically obsolete over time.

---

[1] Reprinted from Wm. E. Souder, "Planning a Career Path from Enginnering to Management," *Engineering Management International*, Vol 4, 1983, pp. 101–129, by permission.

Step 1: Self-assessment. A thorough, candid self-assessment of one's own skills, abilities, interests, aspirations.

Recycle

Step 2: Discussion of results from step 1 with professional counselor and supervisor.

Recycle

Step 3: Determination of life-space and stage goals. Individual determines the specific goals hoped to be achieved at each stage or "space" in life; these may be chronicled by age points, increments of time or other milestone points.

Step 4: Determination of organizational jobs. The population of jobs within the organization are listed and characterized (skill levels required, responsibility levels, training and education needed, etc.).

Step 5: Discussions with professional counselor and supervisor.

Recycle

Step 6: Determination of career goals. Fitting of results from steps 1, 3, and 4 into a career goal plan; the goals should be specified for the short range (one year or less), the intermediate range (one to five years), and the long range (five to fifteen years).

Recycle

Step 7: Acquisition of necessary training and education. Both formal and informal training may be specified, as needed, both on the job and outside; an optimum package will be specified.

Step 8: Monitoring of planned actions.

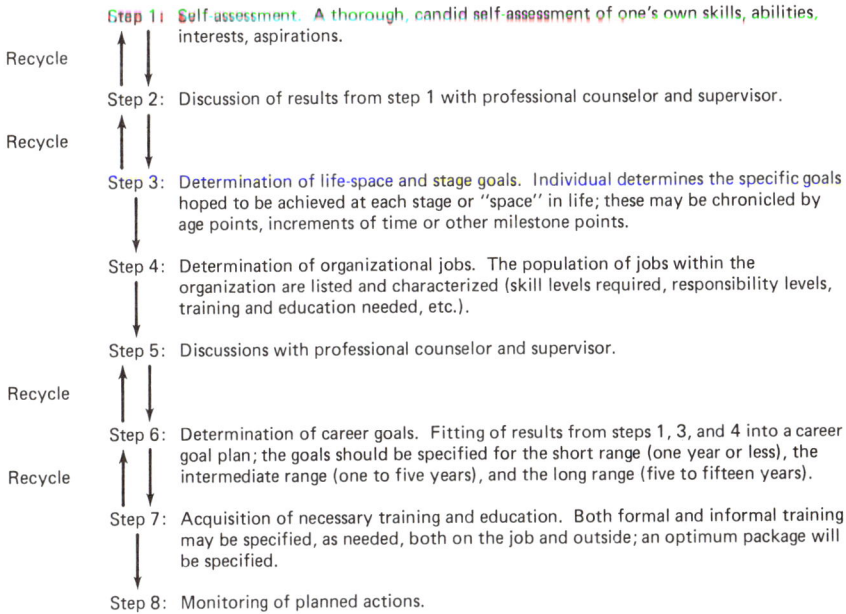

Figure B.1. The career planning process.

B.2. THE CAREER PLANNING PROCESS

The career planning process usually involves the joint efforts of the employee, the supervisor, and a professional career counselor, over a period of several months' time. As outlined in Figure B.1, the complete process consists of eight overlapping steps [1, 2, 5].

Career planning involves considerable hard thinking by all parties. The employee is challenged to be introspective and self-evaluative about family stages, personal wants, and career objectives, as a basis for specifying a life plan and a set of career goals. The professional counselor can play an important role in helping employees with these aspects, through personal interview methods, by administering various skill tests, and by exposing the individual to various literature. The counselor can also help in specifying an optimum training package for each employee. The supervisor can play a helpful and supportive role in acquainting the individual with other jobs within the organization, and in describing the skills required to succeed within each of these jobs.

Though other persons may thus provide assistance, the effectiveness of career planning depends primarily on the initiative of the individual in gathering useful career information, developing valid self-appraisals, setting attainable goals, and defining appropriate pathways. The individual's strengths and weaknesses must be honestly and forthrightly evaluated. Efforts must be made to gather information about alternative jobs and careers. Goals and plans must be kept reasonable and consistent with the individual's capabilities and the available alternative jobs. These plans must be kept flexible, and the individual must be willing to readjust the plans to changing information and circumstances as time passes.

B.3. FROM ENGINEER TO MANAGER

Career planning is important for everyone. It is especially important for the young engineer who wants to move into a management career. Engineers often make good managers. But they must *learn* how to be good managers.

B.3.1. What Is Management?

Management is the art of getting things done through others. In order to effectively work through others, a successful manager must be able to competently perform the seven functions of management listed in Table B.1. Planning, organizing, staffing, directing and controlling are the fundamental functions of management. If any of these five functions are lacking, the management process will not be effective. Note that these are necessary, but they are not *sufficient* functions for managerial effectiveness. Getting things done through people requires the manager to also be effective at motivating and leading others. Note that the relative importance of the seven functions listed in Table B.1 may vary with the *level* of management. Top management success requires an emphasis on planning, organizing and controlling. Middle-level management success often requires great skills in staffing, directing, and leading. Lower-level managers must be especially effective at motivating and leading others.

B.3.2. Engineering versus Management

As Table B.2 shows, the functions of management require a very different set of skills than those normally associated with engineering. Engineering involves hands-on contact with the work. Manager's are always at least one step removed from the work: they can only impact the work through others. An engineer can take personal satisfaction and gratification in his own physical creations, and from the work itself. Managers must learn to be gratified through others and their achievements. Engineering is a science.

Table B.1. The Functions of Management

Planning	Setting goals and objectives and deciding in advance what actions are to be taken. Planning is a process of realistically anticipating future problems, analyzing them, estimating their likely impacts, and determining actions that will lead to the desired outcomes, objectives or goals.
Organizing	Establishing interrelationships between people and things, in such a way that human and material resources are effectively focused toward achieving the goals of the enterprise. Organizing involves grouping activities and people, defining jobs, delegating the appropriate authority to each job, specifying the reporting structure and interrelationships between these jobs, and providing the policies or other means for coordinating these jobs with each other.
Staffing	Manning the various jobs and positions that have been defined by the organizing function. Staffing involves appraising and selecting candidates, setting the compensations and rewards structure for each job, training personnel, conducting performance appraisals, and performing salary administration.
Directing	Guiding and supervising subordinates, and commanding the direction of human and nonhuman resources toward the goals of the enterprise. Directing involves explaining, providing instructions, pointing out proper directions for the future, clarifying assignments, orienting personnel in the most effective directions, and focusing resources.
Motivating	Energizing people to show an inner-directness and enthusiasm in pursuing the goals of the enterprise. Motivating refers to the interpersonal skill to encourage outstanding human performance in others, and to instill in them an inner drive and a zeal to pursue the goals and objectives of various tasks that may be assigned to them.
Leading	Encouraging others to follow the example set for them, with great commitment and conviction. Leading involves setting examples for others, establishing a sense of group pride and spirit, and instilling allegiance.
Controlling	Checking deviations from the plans and taking corrective actions. Controlling involves monitoring achievements and progress against the plans, measuring the degree of compliance with the plans, deciding when a deviation is significant, and taking actions to realign operations with the plans.

Table B.2.   Engineering versus Management.

WHAT ENGINEERS DO	WHAT MANAGERS DO
Minimize risks, emphasize accuracy and mathematical precision	Take calculated risks, rely heavily on intuition, take educated guesses and try to be "about right"
Exercise care in applying sound scientific methods, on the basis of reproducible data	Exercise leadership in making decisions under widely varying conditions, based on sketchy information
Solve technical problems, based on their own individual skills	Solve techno-people problems, based on skills in integrating the talents and behaviors of others
Work largely through their own abilities to get things done	Work through others to get things done

It is characterized by precision, reproducibility, proven theories, and experimentally verifiable results. Management is an art. It is characterized by intuition, studied judgments, unique events, and one-time occurrences. Engineering is a world of things; management is a world of people. People have feelings, sentiments, and motives that may cause them to behave in unpredictable or unanticipated ways. Engineering is based on physical laws, so that most events occur in an orderly, predictable fashion [7].

B.3.3. The Transition from Engineer to Manager

When the engineer enters management, new perspectives must be acquired and new motivations must be found. The engineer must learn to enjoy leadership challenges, detailed planning, helping others, taking risks, making decisions, working through others, and using the organization. In contrast to the engineer, the manager achieves satisfaction from directing the work of others (not things), exercising authority (not technical knowledge), and conceptualizing new ways to do things (not doing them). There are three skills that engineers find most troublesome to acquire. They are: (1) learning to *trust* others, (2) learning how to work *through* others, and (3) learning how to take satisfaction in the work of *others* [6, 7].

The step from engineering to management is a big one. To become successful managers, engineers usually must learn new skills, acquire new values and broaden their perspectives. This takes time, on-the-job and off-the-job training, and careful planning. In short, engineers can become good managers only through effective career planning.

B.4. A TYPICAL PATHWAY

The young engineer who aspires to a management career often lacks the information to develop an effective career plan. What skills should he or she strive to acquire? What assignments will increase his or her managerial skills? What new behavior patterns should be maintained? Should new friends, acquaintances and colleagues be sought out? Are some assignments better stepping stones than others to management jobs?

These questions are typical of the many uncertainties that may confront the young engineer. The answers can vary, depending on the nature of the organization and its culture. However, we can find some answers in the hypothetical case of Ed the Engineer.

B.4.1. Ed the Engineer

Soon after Ed began his engineering job with the XYZ Company it became clear to him that his undergraduate engineering training had prepared him well. Ed had taken all the engineering courses he could, studied hard, and learned well. With the accomplishment of each new technical assignment, his confidence and experience grew. He soon found that his supervisor was delegating more and more authority to him, providing him with increasing decision making responsibilities on many important technical aspects. Ed generally found that he could handle these challenges. However, one problem did arise where his lack of experience failed him. He quickly recognized his inadequacy, sought the advice of several more experienced colleagues, and then conferred with his supervisor on the alternatives that he had been able to develop. Collectively, Ed and his supervisor arrived at a solution. There was another instance where Ed found that he simply did not have the technical know-how to solve the problem, even though his engineering training had been very thorough. A wrong decision could significantly affect the company's future. Ed promptly referred the matter to his supervisor, who decided to assign the problem to the XYZ Company's "think tank" of senior scientists for further research.

From time to time Ed found that his supervisor gave him the responsibility to plan and direct small-scale task forces and projects. These assignments usually included the supervision of some hourly employees and some technicians. Ed noted that he was never asked to supervise anyone whose job he did not understand. In fact, at one time or another during his first few months with the company, Ed had performed most of the tasks he was supervising. In spite of his desire for more challenging supervisory roles, Ed found that there was something new to be learned from each of these assignments. At the end of each day Ed carefully reflected on that day's activities. He thought about how the subordinates reacted to him, and why they behaved in various ways, and he pondered over his effectiveness as a supervisor. Ed recognized that these assignments could mean that he would eventually be given larger supervisory responsibilities, and that this might be the beginning of a management career. Therefore, Ed requested a bi-weekly meeting with his supervisor to discuss the many things he observed, his leadership style, and general management philosophies.

Ed's assignments were not always to his liking. He felt that some of his assignments did not effectively use his talents, while others involved considerable "politics" and protocol. An example was the feeder-scheduling report. This report involved a great deal of tedious time study and hand calculations. It was not clear to Ed how the report was used, or why his supervisor wanted it. But when Ed questioned its value he was abruptly told by his supervisor that "this is the way we do it here, and it's part of your job." Recognizing that he couldn't change the long-standing institution of the feeder-scheduling report, Ed instead sought to ease his part of it by computerizing the calculations. This freed some of his time for more creative activities.

Ed hired into the XYZ Company at about the same time as Mike and Joe, two young engineers with backgrounds and credentials comparable to Ed's. Ed viewed Mike as a "wheeler-dealer" who sometimes took credit for other's ideas, maintained high visibility with management and frequently manipulated others. There was one incident that genuinely disgusted Ed: Mike received a promotion by taking credit for Joe's idea. Joe left the company over this incident. Ed considered exposing Mike. But it occurred to him that Mike had presented the idea in a way that was highly acceptable to management, while Joe had failed to effectively communicate his idea on two previous occasions. Ed pondered at length over this incident. His feelings were a mixture of fear, awe, and disgust. Ed recognized that Joe failed because of his own (Joe's) lack of self-promotional skills. However, Ed felt it was a great loss to the XYZ Company that Joe's creative abilities and Mike's communication skills could not somehow be teamed up. Under the circumstances, Ed felt it would be unprofessional of him to attempt to expose Mike. But he vowed never to be taken advantage of in this fashion. This incident also caused Ed to review his own personal dress code and to reflect on his own communication and self-promotional skills. He decided that wearing a suit and tie occasionally, especially for meetings with top management, couldn't hurt his image.

As he became more familiar with the organization, Ed began to reflect on the various jobs and positions that he became acquainted with. He thought about the skills required for each job, and appraised his own abilities with respect to those requirements. Ed kept a running list of the jobs he might move to next.

Ed sometimes disagreed with the decisions and actions of his colleagues and his superiors. But he felt it was unprofessional to criticize them, unless they asked for his advice. This lesson was brought home to Ed very pointedly one day, when a young engineer publicly criticized a supervisor in a staff meeting. The engineer was, in fact, correct. The supervisor had erred in judgment. But the sense of unprofessionalism and the pallor cast on the meeting by this event was extremely embarrassing to everyone, including Ed.

Ed soon recognized that, though the XYZ Company's approach to management appeared to be effective, he needed to gain a broader perspective in order to more fully develop himself. He worked out a program of study that included attendance at several company-sponsored seminars, selected three-day training programs, and a personal reading program. Ed soon discovered that management was a vast field, and he enrolled in a part-time masters degree program at the local university in order to focus his study.

Ed's supervisory responsibilities began to gradually increase. He found himself supervising increasingly larger subprojects. Sometimes these responsibilities included large budgets and involved many different persons in several different departments. In two cases, the outcome of the work was critical for the future of the company. These experiences brought Ed into decision making contact with many different persons throughout the XYZ Company, affording him opportunities to see how the different parts of the company actually functioned. Ed soon found that his university courses and these job experiences reinforced each other. He began to feel a strong conviction that he should devote himself to a career in management, rather than to a career in the technical aspects of engineering. The XYZ Company had a "dual ladder" or a dual promotional system [3, 4]. Equivalent pay and status could be achieved in either the technical or managerial tracks. But Ed was beginning to feel that he "belonged" in the management track.

On a Monday morning at 9:00 AM, Ed was very surprised to be called into a meeting with his boss and with the Vice President of Engineering. There, he was asked to become the Program Manager of a major development effort, Program Y. Ed enthusiastically accepted.

B.4.2. The Major Lessons

For the young engineer who wants to become a manager, there are seven major lessons to be learned from the story of Ed the Engineer.

1. Your first hurdle is to demonstrate your proficiency as an engineer. A

poor engineer *can* become a good manager. But most poor engineers will never be given the chance to prove they can manage. They will not be viewed as "management stock".

2. Cultivate as many working relationships as you possibly can with more experienced colleagues who can assist you. Call on them when you need help. But don't use them frivolously. The mark of a wise person is knowing when his or her knowledge has been exceeded and other viewpoints are needed. The mark of a successful manager is knowing how to get things done by drawing on the teamwork of others.

3. Work closely with your supervisor. Keep him or her well informed, exchange viewpoints frequently and develop an open dialogue. It is up to you to let your supervisor know if you are not yet ready for the larger, more challenging assignment that has been given to you. You may fear that admitting you can't do it will cause your supervisor to lose faith in you. But have you considered the loss in faith if you take the job, knowing it's beyond your current capabilities, and then you fail at it? Have you considered the impacts of such a failure on the rest of the organization, and on the careers of others?

4. Be patient. You should indeed ask for supervisory responsibilities when you feel you are ready for them. But do not be impatient if the opportunities don't appear as often as you would like, or if your supervisor feels you are not ready yet. There is something to be learned from every assignment.

5. Develop your introspective skills. Learn to empathize. Develop your observational powers. Subtle nuances and behaviors that seem meaningless may add up to important keys to people's behaviors.

6. Expose yourself to as much management theory as you can. Read widely and try to integrate what you read.

7. A management degree does not qualify you to manage anything. A Ph.D. degree may qualify you for a higher-level job than a B.S. degree. But a person with no degrees at all may be a vastly superior manager to another person with a Ph.D. degree in management. The practice of management is a learned art.

These lessons will not be highly palatible to the impatient young engineer. But self-control and disciplined patience are a hallmark of a successful manager.

B.4.3. Other Important Lessons

Like most young engineers, Ed didn't know enough about management during his early years to make an intelligent career choice. He wisely kept his options open while he learned as much as he could about all aspects of management. It is noteworthy that Ed did not fall into the management status trap. In this trap, the young engineer feels compelled to prematurely commit himself to a management career to fulfill his status needs. This may, in part, have been influenced by the fact that the XYZ Company had a dual advancement ladder [3, 4].

Ed realized that there are some politics and undesirable aspects to every job. Instead of complaining, Ed tried to learn something from each situation. He changed what he could and developed a tolerance for things he couldn't change. He strived to always present an image of professional competency. He kept his eyes on his competition: others who were equally capable of advancing to the next job he sought. He maintained a healthy respect for and even fear for his competitors, but he never played unfairly with them.

Even though Ed's knowledge of his capabilities and his career opportunities was meager, he was always forward-thinking. He constantly speculated and planned as best he could on the assignments that might become available and the challenges he sought. All planning is iterative. Ed realized that no one ever has enough information to write a comprehensive, accurate plan on the first try. The first version of the plan may only identify the missing information. As this missing information is sought out and filled in, a sound, well-informed plan will eventually emerge.

There was no professional career counselor available to Ed, but he was able to gain considerable advice and help from his boss and others around him. Every year, hundreds of new books and articles appear on management. Ed availed himself of these as best he could.

Ed recognized that his physical appearance had little bearing on his effectiveness, but it may have a great deal to do with how others view you. Conformity with the suit and tie look is sometimes one of the irritating nuances that one must tolerate in order to advance.

Ed refrained from undue criticism of his colleagues and the work of others. He attempted to present his bosses with solution alternatives along with every problem, maintained a willingness to learn, and listened a great deal. Ed learned a cardinal rule from one incident: never publicly embarrass your supervisor or otherwise tarnish your supervisor's image of his own competency.

B.5. AN ANALYSIS

Though the XYZ Company did not provide any formal career planning, Ed engaged in his own career planning process. He periodically assessed his personal strengths and weaknesses, examined his goals, considered the

Table B.3. Two of Ed's Career Plans.

	AN EARLY PLAN	A LATER REVISION
Self-assessment		
Strengths	Organizing, following up, planning, coordinating	Organizing, following up, planning, directing, leading
Weaknesses	Working with people, motivating others, leading, directing	Working with people, motivating; lack good overall picture of the whole company
Objectives		
Now	Management	To manage the company's resources
Ultimate	?	To make a significant impact on the techno-business thrust of the company
Potential		
Next step	Section head Project coordinator Senior engineer	Program Manager
Potential future jobs	?	Director General manager
Training needs	?	Top management skills, interpersonal skills, decision making methods

available jobs, and discussed these aspects with his supervisor. Two of Ed's career plans are presented in Table B.3. Note that Ed's early career plan (the left side of Table B.3) shows a number of uncertainties about goals, future jobs, and training needs. Ed's early career plan was limited by his relative inexperience within the XYZ Company, and by his rather limited viewpoint of the management profession. By contrast, the later revision shown in the right side of Table B.3 is much more complete. Ed's increasing awareness of his job alternatives and his growing management skills are reflected in this revision. It is especially interesting to note how Ed's perceptions and value orientations changed from the early plan to the later revision. The goal statements in the revision reflect a much more mature, systematic perspective.

Figure B.2 describes Ed's career path from his first job as a staff engineer with the XYZ Company to his promotion to program manager. The path appears to meander somewhat, it crosses both technical and administrative

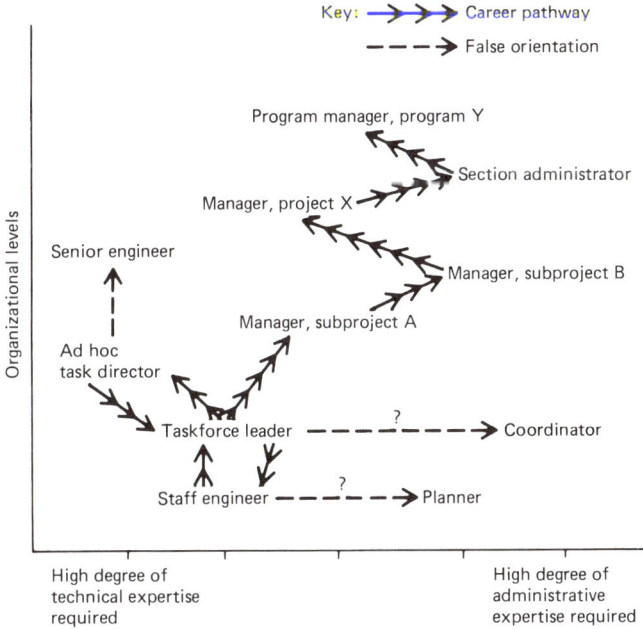

Figure B.2. Trackings of a portion of Ed's career path.

jobs, and it loops between two of the jobs. This is typical of career pathways from engineering to management. In Ed's case, the journey from staff engineer took him through increasingly challenging positions that provide a spectrum of techno-administrative experiences. In the beginning, Ed's pathway looped between the staff engineer, taskforce leader, and task director positions. As his skills grew and his expertise increased, Ed moved on into subproject, project, and major program management responsibilities. The subproject B and section administrator jobs rounded out Ed's skills in administration, preparing him for the program manager role

There were several times when Ed became confused about his future with the XYZ Company. During those times when he was serving as a highly technical ad hoc task director, Ed thought that the XYZ Company management might be preparing him for a technical career, i.e., promotion to senior engineer and on to senior scientist. When he was serving as a staff engineer and as a taskforce leader, it seemed to him that the next logical progression would take him to the coordinator or planner jobs. Both of these pathways would move him up the administrative ladder. This seemed to be confirmed when Ed was promoted to section administrator.

Ed's meandering career path and his uncertainties about his future with the XYZ Company are the typical experiences in most companies. In spite of these problems, Ed succeeded in becoming a candidate for a top management job.

Ed was lucky. He succeeded in spite of the lack of a systematic career planning system at the XYZ Company. In many cases, good potential managers become lost in meandering pathways, become discouraged and leave the company, or incorrectly pursue one of their false orientations when there is no career planning. The consequent misdirection and loss of human talent to the organization and the unfulfillment of the victimized individuals are inexcusable costs. The cost of setting up and administering an in-company career path system is miniscule when compared to these costs.

B.6. CONCLUSIONS

In order to become successful managers, engineers must learn new skills, acquire new values and reorient their thinking. Many good engineers have become successful managers, and there are established career pathways from engineering to management. However, the transition from engineering to

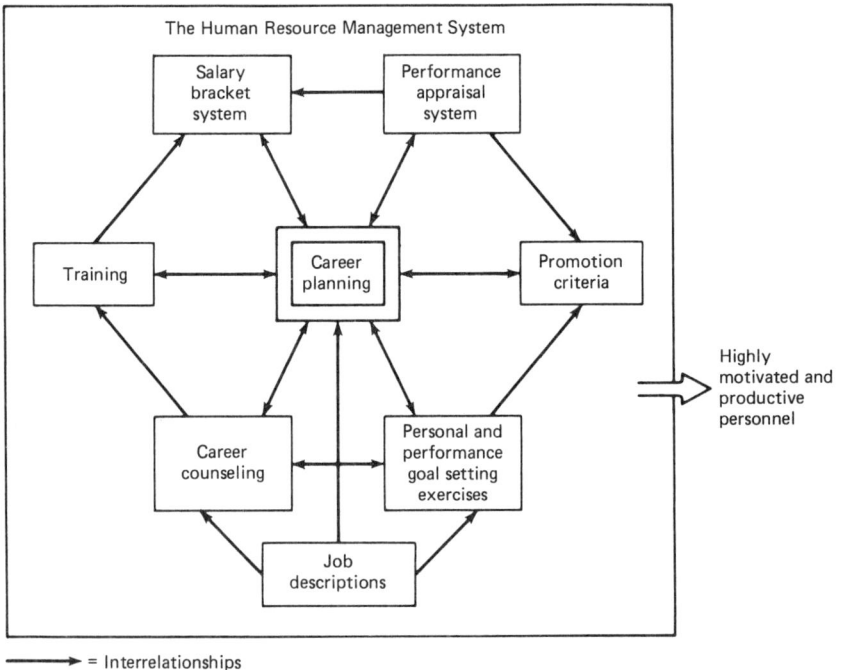

Figure B.3. The systems approach to career planning.

management requires time for the individual to mature, a progression of on-the-job experiences, and careful career planning.

Career planning is best viewed as part of a total human resource management system: a system consisting of regular goal-setting exercises, regular performance appraisals, adequate training, and continuous career counseling. Career planning becomes most effective where a variety of jobs and pathways are provided by the organization, the performance requirements for these jobs are made explicit, the criteria for promotions are spelled out, and the salary brackets are kept consistent with this information. The interrelationships between career planning and these other aspects are depicted in Figure B.3.

However, as we have seen here in the hypothetical case of Ed the engineer, useful career planning *can* be carried out without the systems approach depicted in Figure B.3. But the systems approach makes career planning much more effective, and generally assists the engineer in making a better transition to management. In the case of Ed the engineer, the systems approach could have substantially reduced his uncertainties, moved him more swiftly along the pathways, and eliminated many of his false orientations.

B.7. REFERENCES

1. Souder, W. E., "The Career Planning, Development and Counseling Process: A Systems Approach," working draft or presentation, October 15, 1980.
2. Glueck, W. F. *Personnel: A Diagnostic Approach*. Business Publications: Plano, Texas, 1982, pp. 271–277.
3. Kimblin, C. W. and W. E. Souder, "Maintaining Staff Productivity as Half-Life Decreases," *Research Management*, Vol. XVII, No. 6, November 1975, pp. 29–35.
4. Moore, D. C. and D. S. Davies, "The Dual Ladder: Establishing and Operating It," *Research Management*, July 1977, Vol. 20, No. 4, pp. 14–19.
5. Burack, E. H. "Career Paths—Why All the Confusion?" *Human Resource Management*, 1977, pp. 21–27.
6. Badawy, M. K. *Developing Managerial Skills in Engineers and Scientists*. New York: Van Nostrand-Reinhold, 1982.
7. Souder, W. E. *Management Decision Methods for Managers of Engineering and Research*, New York: Van Nostrand-Reinhold, 1980, pp. 9–11.

Index